S0-BXX-805

GLASS

MATERIAL MATTERS

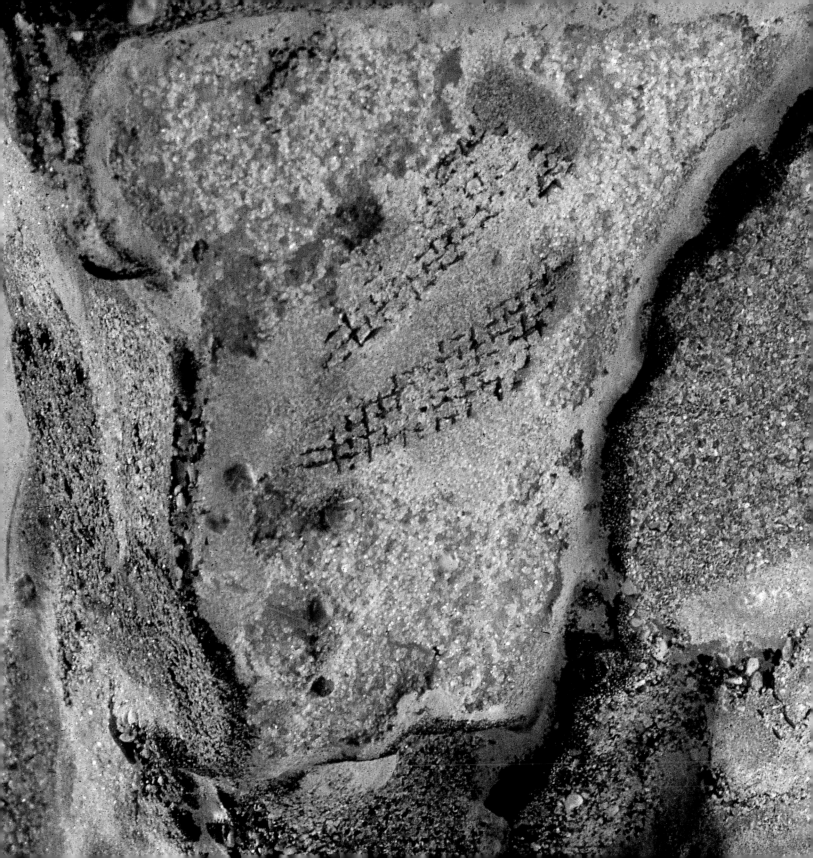

GLASS

MATERIAL

essay by

HOWARD N. FOX

MATTERS

exhibition organized by

HOWARD N. FOX
Curator of Contemporary Art
Los Angeles County Museum of Art

and

SARAH NICHOLS
Chief Curator and Curator of Decorative Arts
Carnegie Museum of Art, Pittsburgh

LOS ANGELES COUNTY MUSEUM OF ART

This volume was published in conjunction with the exhibition **Glass: Material Matters** at the Los Angeles County Museum of Art from April 30 to December 10, 2006.

This exhibition was organized by the Los Angeles County Museum of Art and was made possible by Susan Steinhauser and Daniel Greenberg.

It was supported in part by the Glass Alliance of Los Angeles. Additional support was provided by Ruth C. Greenberg, Roberta and Melvin Ulshansky, Cynthia and Jeffrey Manocherian, The Jon and Mary Shirley Foundation, Dale and Doug Anderson, Andy and Charles Bronfman, Salli and Bernie Harris, Ellie and Mark Lainer, and Dr. Susan Krevoy and Leo Spiwak.

Opening night sponsors: Saul E. Levi and Marsha N. Levine

Published by
Los Angeles County
Museum of Art
5905 Wilshire Boulevard
Los Angeles, CA 90036
© 2006 Museum Associates
All rights reserved.

ISBN: 0-87587-195-X
Library of Congress Control Number:
2005930119

Directors of publications:
Nola Butler and Thomas Frick
Editor: Thomas Frick
Designer: Amy McFarland
Principal photographers:
Steve Oliver and Peter Brenner
Production coordinator:
Karen Knapp
Rights and reproductions
coordinator: Cheryle Robertson
Rights and reproductions
associate: Piper Severance
Proofreader: Dianne Woo

Printed by Arti Grafiche Amilcare Pizzi s.p.a., Milan, Italy

Bank Gothic and Franklin Gothic Condensed, the display types used in this book, were drawn by Morris Fuller Benton (1872–1948), a hugely prolific designer for the American Type Founders Company. American Type Founders was established in 1892 through the merger of twenty-three smaller companies, and Benton, charged with creating a unified type library from these disparate sources, developed the concept of type "families," a basic organizing principle to this day. Benton designed around two hundred typefaces of great diversity, more than anyone else in the precomputer age, and many of them are still in wide use. He was also responsible for some of the most successful revivals in typographic history, including modern interpretations of Bodoni and Garamond. Benton designed the Franklin Gothic family between 1903 and 1912. It may have been named after Benjamin Franklin, an early American printer, though there is no structural or historical relation to him or his work. The square capitals of Bank Gothic, designed in 1930, show the influence of the Bauhaus and its interest in geometric forms.

Lucas de Groot, a Dutch designer working in Berlin, created the large type family known as TheMix, from which the body text used here was taken. Unusual for its combination of sans-serif capitals and ascenders with serifs, TheMix became widely known when the October 1995 edition of *Wired* magazine was completely set in this family. Perhaps due to the capitalization of nouns in German, de Groot is especially attentive to the delicate balance required in the design of small capitals.

Illustration Credits

Most photographs are reproduced courtesy of the creators, lenders, or photographers of the images depicted. For certain artworks we have been unable to trace copyright holders. We would appreciate notification of same for acknowledgement in future editions. Unless otherwise noted, photography of artwork reproduced in this publication is © 2006 Museum Associates/LACMA.

Front cover, 2 (details), 80, 81: © Lynda Benglis/VAGA, New York; 1 (detail), 112, 113: © Anthony Cragg; 3 (detail), 68: © Stanislav Libenský/Jaraslava Brychtová; 4 (detail), 36, 37: © Joel Philip Myers; 5 (detail), 74: © Diane Hobson; 6–7 (detail), 45: © Toots Zynsky, photo © 2005 Museum Associates/LACMA, by Peter Harholdt; 9 (detail), 24: © Thomas Patti, photo courtesy of the artist; 10 (detail), 48: © Pae White, photo courtesy of Gallery 1301 PE; 11 (detail), 88: © Robert Willson; 12 (detail), 136–9: © Michael Glancy, photo © Gene Dwiggins, Providence; 13 (detail), 78: © Jack Wax; 16: © Věra Lišková; 23: © Larry Bell; 25: © Thomas Patti, photo courtesy of Heller Gallery; 27: Lino Tagliapietro; 28 left: © Jessica Loughlin; 28 right: © Christopher Wilmarth, photo © Carnegie Museum of Art, by Tom Little; 29: © Toshio Iezumi; 31: © Harvey Littleton; 32: © Dale Chihuly; 33: © Dale Chihuly, photo by Dick Busher; 34: © Laura de Santillana, photo © 2005 Museum Associates/LACMA, by Joseph Coscia; 35:© Laura de Santillana; 39–43: © Klaus Moje; 44: © Toots Zynsky, photo courtesy of the artist; 47: © Jorge Pardo; 50–2, 54: © Marquis; 53: © Marquis, photo © 2005 Museum Associates/ LACMA, by Peter Harholdt; 56: © Joey Kirkpatrick/Flora Mace, photo © 2005 Museum Associates/ LACMA, by Peter Harholdt; 57: © Dan Dailey; 59: © Dan Dailey, photo © Bill Truslow; 60: © Hank Murta Adams; 61: © Flo Perkins; 63: © Howard Ben Tré; 64: © Howard Ben Tré, photo © Ric Murray; 65: © Daniel Clayman; 66: © František Vizner; 67: © František Vizner; photo courtesy of Heller Gallery; 69: © Stanislav Libenský/Jaraslava Brychtová, photo courtesy of Heller Gallery; 71–3: © Karla Trinkley; 75: © Diane Hobson; 76, back cover (detail): © Ivan Mareš; 77: © Ivan Mareš; photo courtesy of Heller Gallery; 83: © William Morris; 84–5: © William Morris; 86: © Seth Randall; 89: © Bert Vallien, photo © 2005 Museum Associates/LACMA, by Peter Harholdt; 90: © Bert Vallien; 91: © Jay Musler; 92 left: © Jay Musler; 92 right: © Robert Carlson; 94: © Stanislaw Borowski; 96–8: © Ginny Ruffner; 100: © Richard Meitner, photo courtesy of Barry Friedman Ltd.; 101: © Richard Meitner, photo © 2005 Museum Associates/LACMA, by Joseph Coscia; 102: © Ann Wolff; 104: © Einar and Jamex de la Torre, photo © Fisher Gallery, University of Southern California; 105: © Einar and Jamex de la Torre, photo © Marcus Gonzales and Julio Orozco; 107–8: © Sylvia Levenson; 109: © Judith Schaechter, photo © Carnegie Museum of Art; 111: © Wim Delvoye, courtesy of Sperone Westwater, NY; 114: © Michael Aschenbrenner; 116: © Clifford Rainey; 117: © Clifford Rainey, photo courtesy of Richard Sloan; 118: © Kiki Smith, courtesy of Pac Wildenstein, photo courtesy Shoshana Wayne Gallery; 120: © Kiki Smith, courtesy of Pace Wildenstein; 122: © Rita McBride, photo © Orcutt & Van Der Putten, courtesy of Alexander & Bonin, New York; 124–5: © Therman Statom; 128–9: © Sherrie Levine; 130: © Josiah McElheny, photo © Zindman/Fremont; 132–3: © Jill Reynolds, © Carnegie Museum of Art, by Peter Harholdt; 135: © Michael Glancy; 141: © Bruce Nauman/Artists Rights Society (ARS), New York; 144–5: © Dale Chihuly, photo by Terry Rishel; 148: © JCDA, photo © JCDA/Brian Gulick; 149: © Smith-Miller + Hawkinson, photo © Erieta Attali; 152: © Eric Owen Moss Architects, photo by Tom Bonan; 153: © Foster and Partners, photo by Nigel Young/Foster and Partners; 154: © Renzo Piano Building Workshop (RPBW), by Hays Davidson and John McLean; 156–7: © Rem Koolhaas (OMA/AMO), photo © Philippe Ruault; 158: © Zaha Hadid Architects

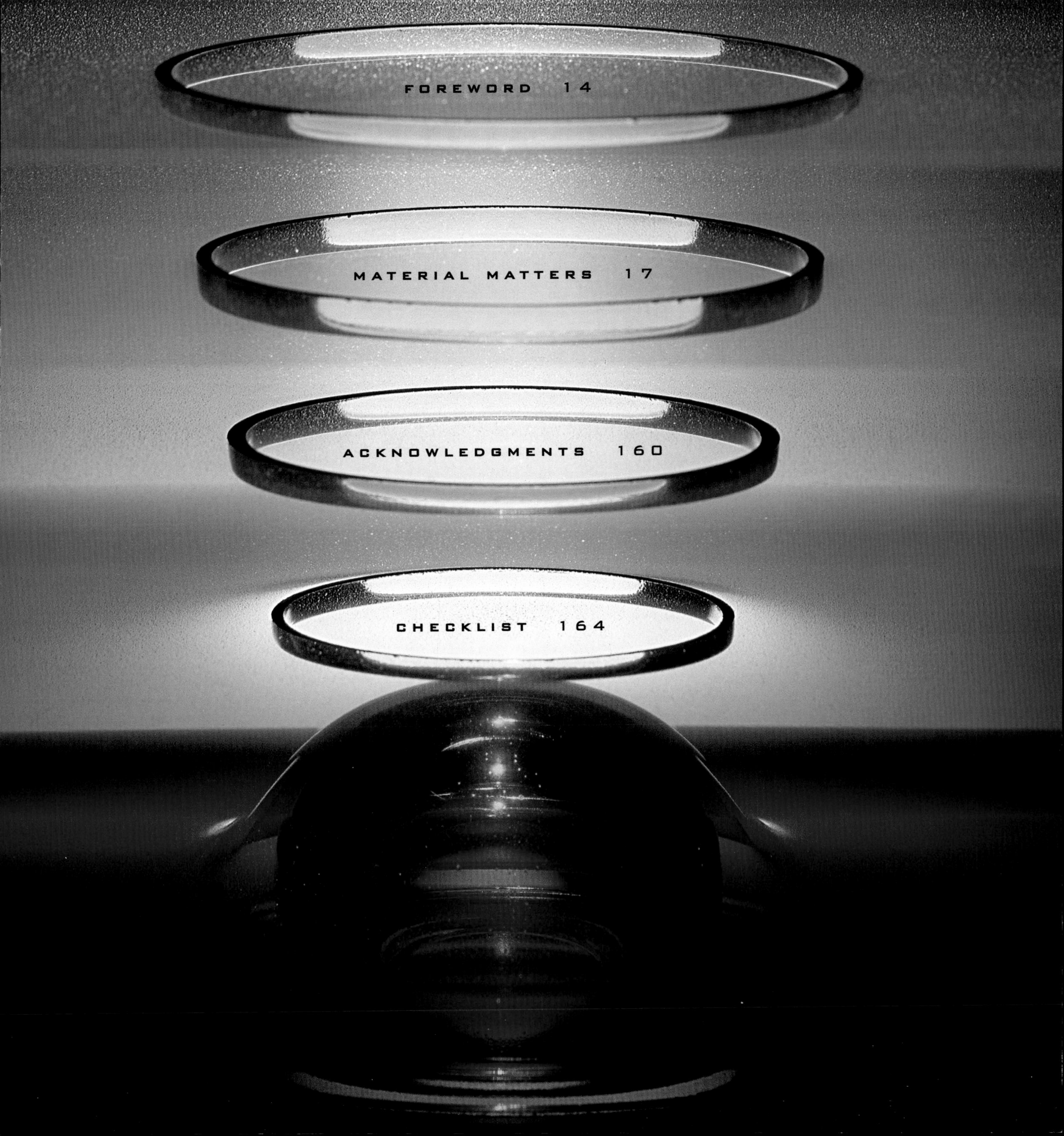

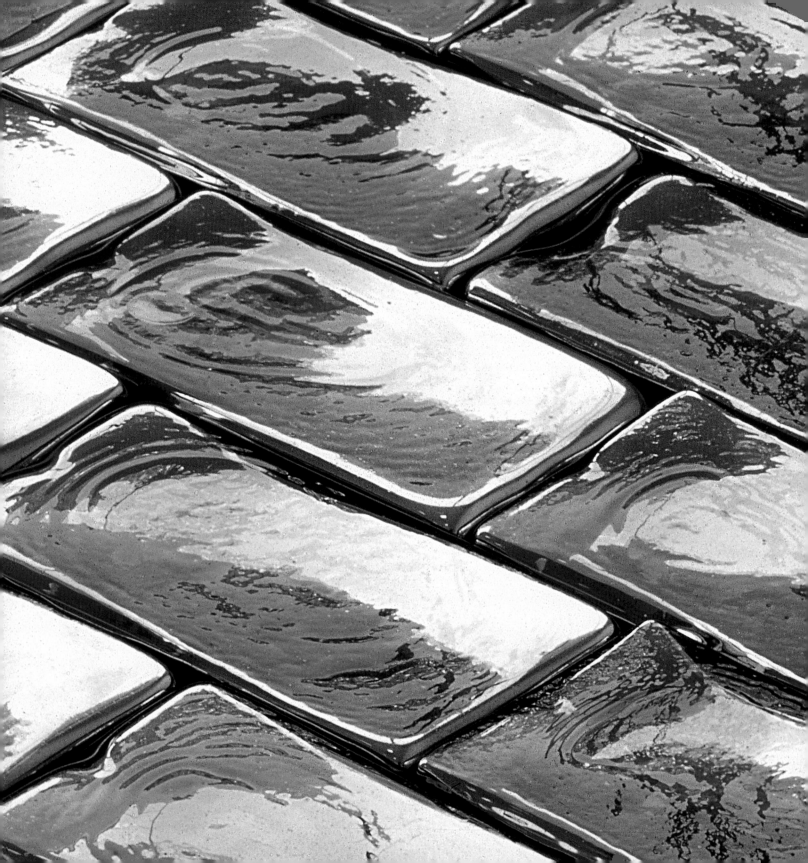

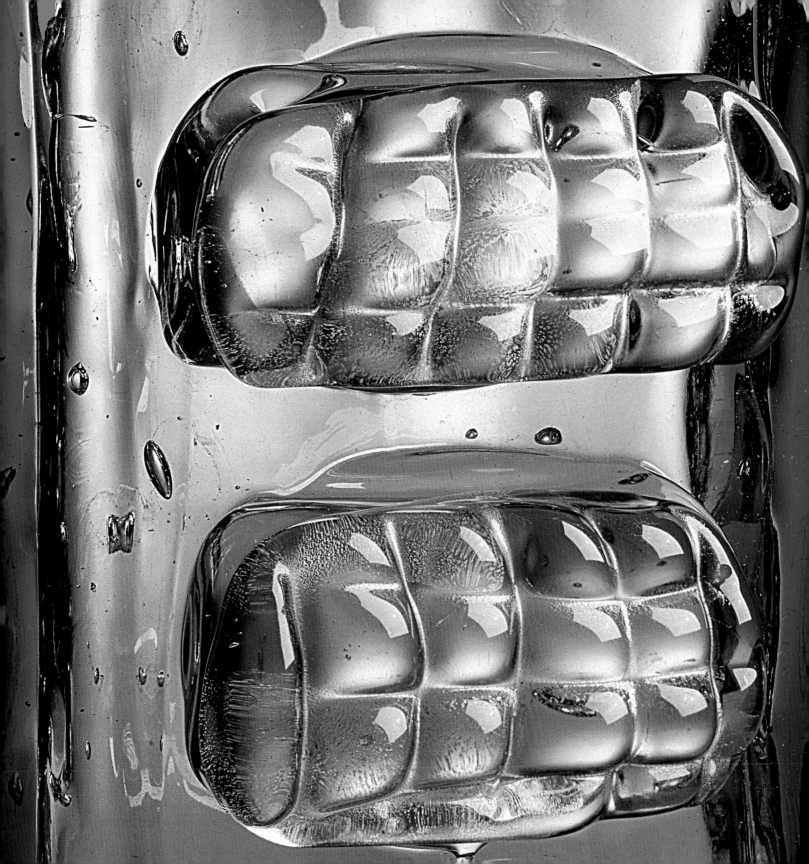

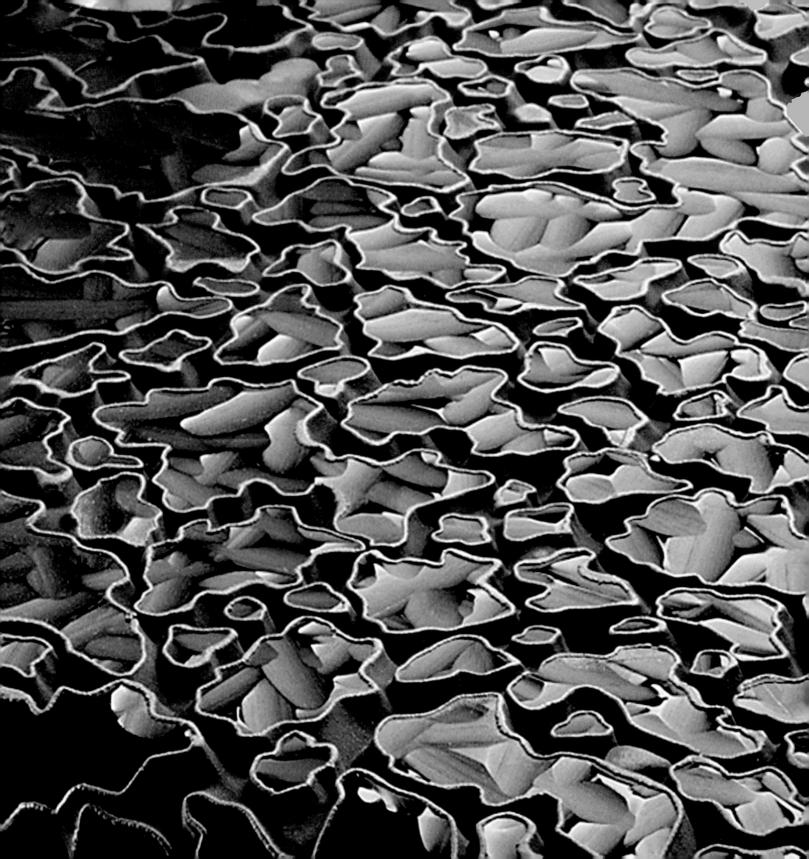

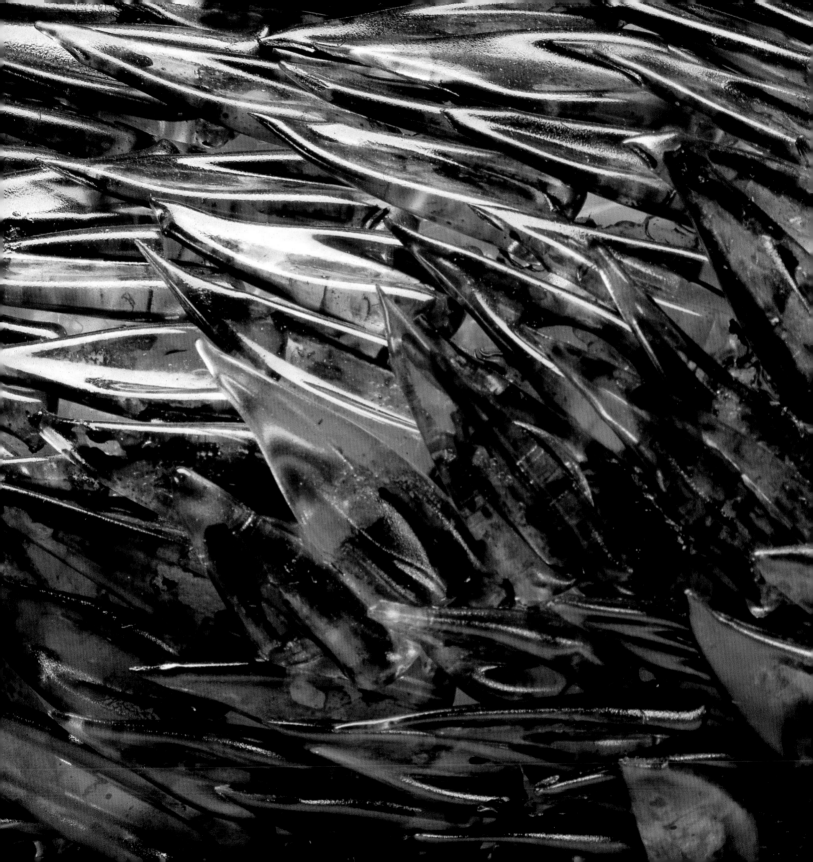

FOREWORD

Glass: Material Matters is the first exhibition of contemporary glass art organized by the Los Angeles County Museum of Art and is one of the first presentations anywhere to explore the artistic use of glass across a diverse range of decorative objects, sculpture, conceptual art, and architecture in a single exhibition. In a highly selective overview, this exhibition showcases a dazzling display of virtuoso technique and bravura formal innovation, all in one medium. In its inclusiveness, the show challenges the viability of distinctions that historians, critics, and curators have traditionally drawn to segregate diverse artistic pursuits that are in fact unified in their preoccupation with glass.

This is a consciously eclectic presentation, organized to reflect a spectrum of thematic, formal, and technical directions in glass primarily from the mid-1980s to the present. Some artists create works of pure geometrical form; others make masks and totemic objects that appear archaeological in origin. A decorative impulse is the primary inspiration for some of the artists, while an exploration of the human body is the focus for others. Some artists working in glass are conceptual artists. Several works, represented photographically in the exhibition galleries, are vast site-specific installations in glass. And the architects in this show, also represented photographically, work on a truly monumental scale.

By offering an overview of the range of artistic possibilities in glass, the show also underscores LACMA's commitment to the collection and display of contemporary works of all kinds in this medium. Approximately half of the more than one hundred works in the exhibition have been selected from LACMA's impressive permanent collection of contemporary glass, which is shared by the departments of contemporary art and decorative art. In addition, the exhibition draws upon some of the finest private collections of glass in the United States.

Glass: Material Matters is a rich offering, with much for the eye and the mind's eye.

Bruce Robertson
Deputy Director, Art Programs
Los Angeles County Museum of Art

Věra Lišková, **Music**, 1980

GLASS

MATERIAL MATTERS

Glass is one of the most ancient of all artistic mediums; it is also one of the most contemporary. For more than three millennia (some say more than five), glass has been an essential aspect of material and visual culture in Western civilization. It is omnipresent in all modern civilizations in everything from stemware to spectacles to skyscrapers.

Glass is surely the most multifarious of mediums. A pencil or crayon may be capable of delineating any image, any subject, any texture or atmosphere that the imagination can conceive, but as materials, graphite or charcoal or chalk always look the same. Bronze can be cast and marble carved into an infinite number of shapes, but bronze or marble as materials always present the same physical properties to the artist's hand or the viewer's eye. Oil paint can convey any picture or abstract image that the artist makes, but the material is always pigment in a supporting medium. Unlike any of these, glass qua glass—as a material in itself—can assume an extraordinary range of physical properties and appearances.

17

Glass is defined by physicists as an "amorphous solid," completely lacking large-scale crystalline order. In fact, it is considered to be the most structurally disordered type of solid known, one whose molecules do not organize as crystals but remain in a state of "dynamic arrest." Perhaps this molecular disorganization is what gives glass its extraordinary malleability. It can be stretched into the lithest arabesque, or blown into the most delicate teardrops and globes, or huffed and puffed into bulbous grotesques. It can be gossamer thin, spun into fibers that can be woven into fabric and made into insulation or draperies, or it can be massively heavy or severely rigid. It can be perfectly transparent, ravishingly hued, glowingly translucent, or as opaque as steel. With recent technical developments in architectural engineering, glass can even appear limpid and sheer while it offers load-bearing strength to actually support buildings. "Dynamic arrest" hardly describes glass's true protean nature.

With such extraordinary material and formal potentials, glass would seem to be ideally suited to many of the values and aspirations of modern art and the premium it placed on innovation. From the moment of modernism's most radical expression, in the early twentieth-century Russian avant-garde, proponents of "a new art for a new epoch" such as Vladimir Tatlin, Antoine Pevsner, and Kasimir Malevich called for a renunciation of traditionalist attitudes and practice. Along with this went a brave embrace of new abstract art forms and the deployment of nontraditional industrial materials with which to realize them. El Lissitzky imagined monuments made not of bronze or marble but of steel—the same substance that would be used to build the modern "sky-scraping" towers he envisioned. Tatlin used manufactured goods like rope and pulleys in his constructions and zealously endorsed an industrial aesthetic. Even the cubists—far more tame, and devoted to the representation (albeit quite abstracted) of traditional subject matter—invented the art form of collage, incorporating such novel materials as newspaper text, theater tickets, and printed oilcloth into their compositions. Pevsner and constructivist sculptor Naum Gabo were among the first artists to use plastic and stainless steel in their art; by the 1970s Donald Judd frequently used concrete, plexiglass, and plywood in his minimalist constructions. But when it came to glass as a primary medium, there was curiously little to be found in mainstream modern art—with the famously conspicuous exception of Marcel Duchamp's **The Bride Stripped Bare by her Bachelors, Even** (1915–23), also known as **The Large Glass**—until well into the 1970s and 1980s.

The reasons can only be surmised. Radical modern artists, with their insistence on the literal, nonillusionistic use of materials and their distrust of ornamentation—together with their demand of avant-garde "progress"—likely found glass, with its chameleon nature, its decorative-art history, and its inescapable associations with past glories—from Venetian glass of the Renaissance to the Galerie des Glaces at the neoclassical Versailles Palace, to the Victorian Crystal Palace—antithetical to their very aims. Whatever the case, the fact remains that until relatively recently, artists working in glass and those employing other mediums did not much explore one another's territory. For most of the modern period, the visual art world has had tacit, and sometimes highly articulated, prejudices against the decorative-art world, whose practice it often derides as "artsy" and "craftsy"; and the decorative art branch of contemporary practice tends to regard its counterparts as academic and elitist.

The so-called studio glass movement in the United States, which began to coalesce in the late 1960s and early 1970s around such figures as Harvey Littleton and Dale Chihuly, was a pivotal chapter in the recent history of glass art that was inspired somewhat by the mutual suspicion between the two camps. Before this movement, there were designers of glass, employed by companies such as Steuben, which turned out editioned objects produced by anonymous artisans. The studio glass movement, by contrast, valorized the role of the designer and the role of the fabricator in a single person—the *artist*—just as we customarily accord a painter or a sculptor respect as the *creator* of the painting or the sculpture. The ideology of the movement was to eliminate the cultural hierarchy between fine art and decorative art, to promulgate respect for the unique handmade object. The studio glass movement did help raise consciousness about contemporary glass art, and in the last decade or so glass has become very well established as an artistic pursuit. Works in glass by important artists generate significant critical and popular response and are the basis of noted private and public collections. The "revo-lution" of studio glass three decades ago is now acknowledged history.

Still, the mutual suspicion lingers, and some old fences continue to divide contemporary artistic practice. In a period of art history that has moved on from discussions of "postmodern" and even "post-postmodern" to a global regard for contemporary art practice in all mediums, from traditional object making to interactive digital forms, and during a period when even the most rigid national and ideological borders are increasingly permeable to inhabi-tants and adherents in all quarters, it seems reactionary and pointless to maintain this state of artistic apartheid. With so many artists working in glass, in styles that range from assertively decorative objects to conceptual art to installation and architecture, it is illuminating to look over the tops of those fences and to find the affinities and confluences that inform so much disparate creativity.

SOME ARTISTS find glass an apt medium in which to evoke an almost Platonic purity of form. The very title of Věra Lišková's **Music** (p. 16) suggests an artistic expression that is itself immaterial. The work is a composition of the most trans-parent and graceful curves, whose arcs recall graphs of mathematical equa-tions. Even if no actual equation is embodied in the work (as there is in cer-tain sculptures by, say, Naum Gabo or Max Bill), Lišková plainly alludes to such formal underpinnings in her ethereal blown glass forms as well as to the geometry of laboratory glassware, which always fascinated her.

21

Larry Bell's art also has affinities with science, and like Lišková, he seems to have been drawn to glass for its apparent immateriality. At the same moment when East Coast artists like Richard Serra, Donald Judd, and Carl Andre were working with such blatantly rough and rugged materials as lead, Cor-Ten steel, concrete, or massive square timbers to produce works of profound, nearly assaultive presence, Los Angeles–based Bell was making intimately scaled, geometrically precise cubes and boxes from thin panes of dichroic glass—that is, glass that is chemically and thermally treated to deposit a tinted film that shimmers with spectral color. These coatings, originally developed to reduce glare in optics and airplane windshields, confer a mysterious light and lightness to Bell's cubes that, seen from certain angles, appear to dematerialize. His **Cube**, made in 1966, is the earliest work in this exhibition.

Like Larry Bell, Thomas Patti often constructs cubes or other rectangular volumes. But where Bell's cubes are hollow, and his colors are on the surface, Patti's sculptures, such as **Starfire Four-Ringed Echo with Azurlite, Red, and Green** (p. 24), often display an architectural structure. Indeed they are constructions, built of layers of industrial glass slabs. He introduces pigments within the strata, heats them until they fuse, and while the mass is still very hot, injects air into it, which forms hollow spheres or rings within. The resulting sculptures, combining the nearly opposed techniques of fusing and blowing

Larry Bell, **Cube**, 1966

Thomas Patti, **Starfire Four-Ringed Echo with Azurlite, Red, and Green**, 1994

Thomas Patti, **Modulated Gray with Orange, Blue, Green**, 2002

glass, reveal a process of formation and coloration stopped in time—a chore-ography carefully poised between stasis and motion. The gracefully swelling, slender form of Lino Tagliapietra's **Boat** suggests a canoe or a gondola gliding silently across the surface of the calmest water. But it is not a representation of a boat, even a highly stylized one. It is purely an abstract shape, and, like all of Tagliapietra's art, it derives from the most elegant and simple geometries, incarnate in the curvaceous fluidity of hot worked glass.

Jessica Loughlin's **Vertical Views 12** (p. 28) consists of two nearly identical planks of off-white glass, with inlaid panels, that hang side by side on a wall and bow ever so slightly outward. There are color and textural differences between these inlays, but they are subtle and in certain light almost indis-cernible. In virtually any gallery space, and in homes with white walls, the physical presence of the work is merely a suggestion, whose materiality is conveyed almost entirely by subtle shifts of color among the object and its environs and the faintest whisper of a shadow. In the upper part of the right-hand panel is engraved a nearly invisible text. With its elegant spareness, Loughlin's work engages the acuity of the beholder's perception, as well as the desire for comprehension.

Christopher Wilmarth's **Gnomon's Parade (Place)** (p. 28) is similarly austere in its simple geometry, though the juxtaposition of the velvety acid-etched glass and the ruggedness of the twisting dark steel column creates not only a material contrast but a visual one. A gnomon is the raised shaft of a sundial

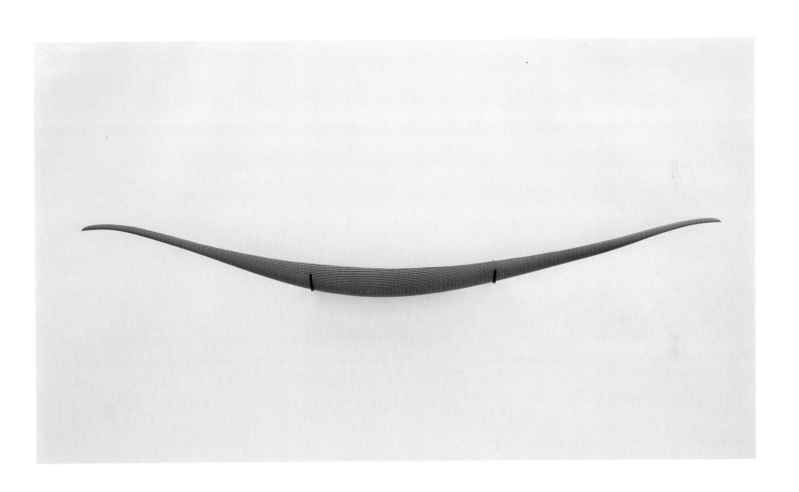

Lino Tagliapietra, **Boat**, 1998

Jessica Loughlin, **Vertical Views 12**, 2001

Christopher Wilmarth, **Gnomon's Parade (Place)**, 1980

that casts the moving shadow. Wilmarth's allusions to the sun, to light and darkness, and to the passage of time imbue this static but visually dynamic work with astronomical associations. Toshio Iezumi's solid glass discs and shallow craterlike shapes, such as **Ring of Water**, display an obvious weightiness. However, the glass he mixes, while not crystal clear, has a somber clarity. The perfection of simple geometric forms, the density of material, and the silvery gray light within the glass project a Zenlike quietude and spirituality, which are important aspects of traditional as well as much contemporary Japanese art.

Toshio Iezumi, **Ring of Water**, 1995

TRANSPARENCY

is a perpetually fascinating allure of glass. But so is its ability to embody the most vibrant or subtle colorations, in almost any degree of translucency or opacity. The ability of glass to apparently materialize pure color in almost any shape attracts artists who seem to want to "paint" three-dimensionally. If we extend the definition of *paint* from pigment suspended in a medium such as oil or acrylic base to include pigment suspended in molten silica, which is glass before it cools, then there are some glass artists who must qualify simultaneously as painters and sculptors.

Harvey Littleton's looping and twisting sculptures are formed from concentric strata of variously colored bands often cased in an outer layer of utterly limpid glass. His works appear to harness pure color, and while they are formally very fluid, there is a precision to his workmanship that gives them a nearly mathematical exactitude.

Dale Chihuly, certainly one of the most noted of contemporary artists, is best known for the ebullient flourish of his grand chandeliers and ceilings, such as at the Bellagio Hotel in Las Vegas. His early work was quite different, although it did provide the impetus for much of what would follow. **Basket Cylinder** (p. 32) is a modestly scaled vessel in yellow, punctuated by included stripes and squiggles of green, red, and other hues. An early example of studio glass, it asserts its handmade qualities through slight imperfections and the apparently gestural dynamics of its painterly design; this is no genteel, manufactured object, but a one-of-a-kind composition whose elemental

Harvey Littleton, **Red/Blue Combination Arc**, 1984

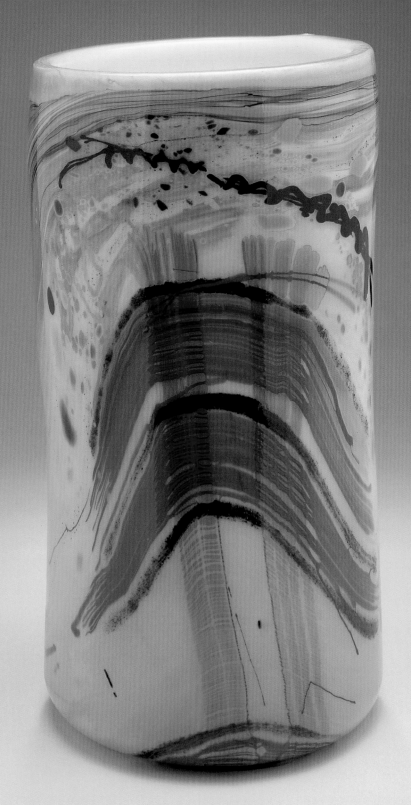

Dale Chihuly, **Basket Cylinder**, c. 1976

geometric form serves as a "canvas" for manipulating color in the medium of glass. Through the years Chihuly's forms became increasingly more active and undulating—the contemporary equivalent of rococo—and his use of radiant color launched into truly virtuosic display. Rather than working in simple geometries, by the 1980s Chihuly was basing much of his art on natural forms; but again, color and tone have the starring role.

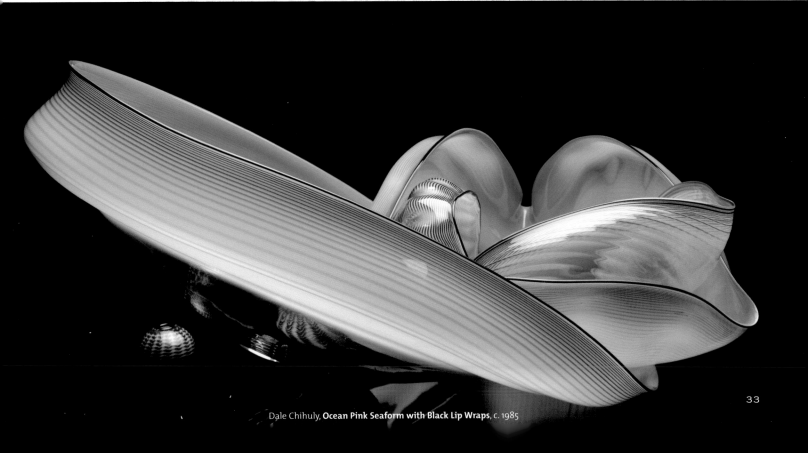

Dale Chihuly, **Ocean Pink Seaform with Black Lip Wraps**, c. 1985

Laura de Santillana, **Dawn III**, 2002

Laura de Santillana comes from a family of Italian glassblowers and is a master of traditional glass techniques. However, many observers associate her art with the paintings of Mark Rothko. Often de Santillana makes square or rectangular hollow vessels that are crossed horizontally with bands of glowing color, which dissolve into lightly tinted glass. Her compositions are faintly reminiscent of Rothko's, as is the luminosity of her colors. Not surprisingly, the spiritual content that has been attributed to his work has likewise been attributed to hers. Joel Philip Myers creates abstract compositions

Laura de Santillana, **Mud**, 2001

Joel Philip Myers, **Cforangeredksg**, 1988

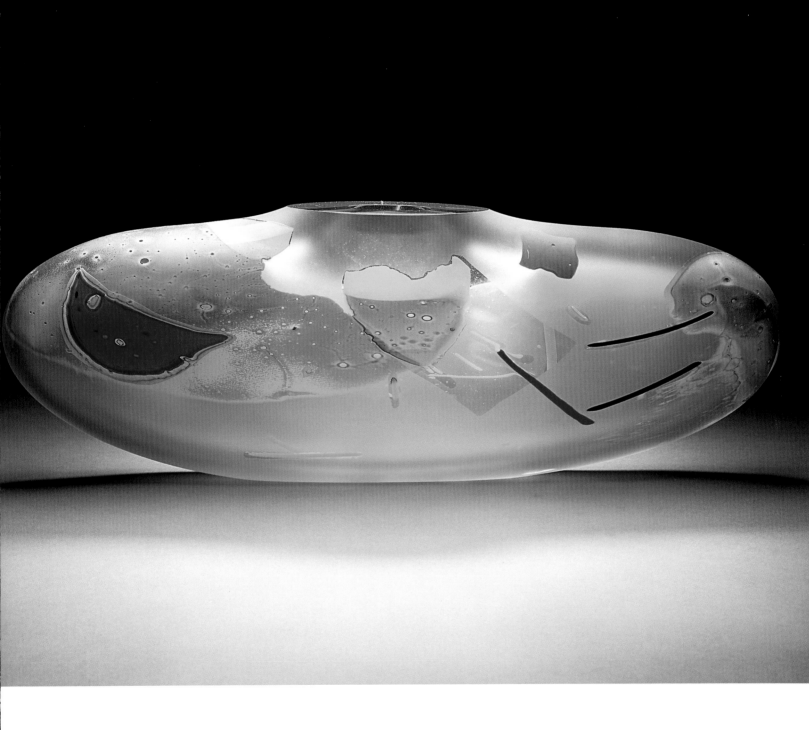

Joel Philip Myers, **Cfbyekkksg**, 1984

such as **Cforangeredksg** (p. 36), and his works might also be aptly compared to certain kinds of abstract painting. Such comparisons are fair, but Chihuly, de Santillana, and Myers are working in a mode that has its own centuries-long tradition. They are not imitating painting but exploring the inherent coloristic possibilities of glass.

The German-born Australian Klaus Moje has focused on the forms of the bowl and the plate for much of his recent career. But these bowls and plates are meant to contain and to serve nothing except visual pleasure (pp. 39–43). Moje's forms are constructed of fused opaque glass pieces that are heated so that they partially melt, slumping in molds whose shape they assume, and then finished with varied techniques. Their surfaces, together with the opacity and special pigmentation of the glass stock, produce some of the most piercingly vivid colors in glass work today. His match may be met in the art of Toots Zynsky. Her constructions cross boundaries between cast and fused glass. Working with ravishingly colored glass rods, each about the thickness of a strand of angel-hair pasta, she bundles and shapes them while they are hot enough to slump but not to melt. Instead, they fuse to form a single object—usually a bowl-like vessel composed of thousands of still-perceptible individual filaments. The effect of the brilliantly colored rods, in such works as **Chaos in Paradise** (p. 45), makes the form seem aflame.

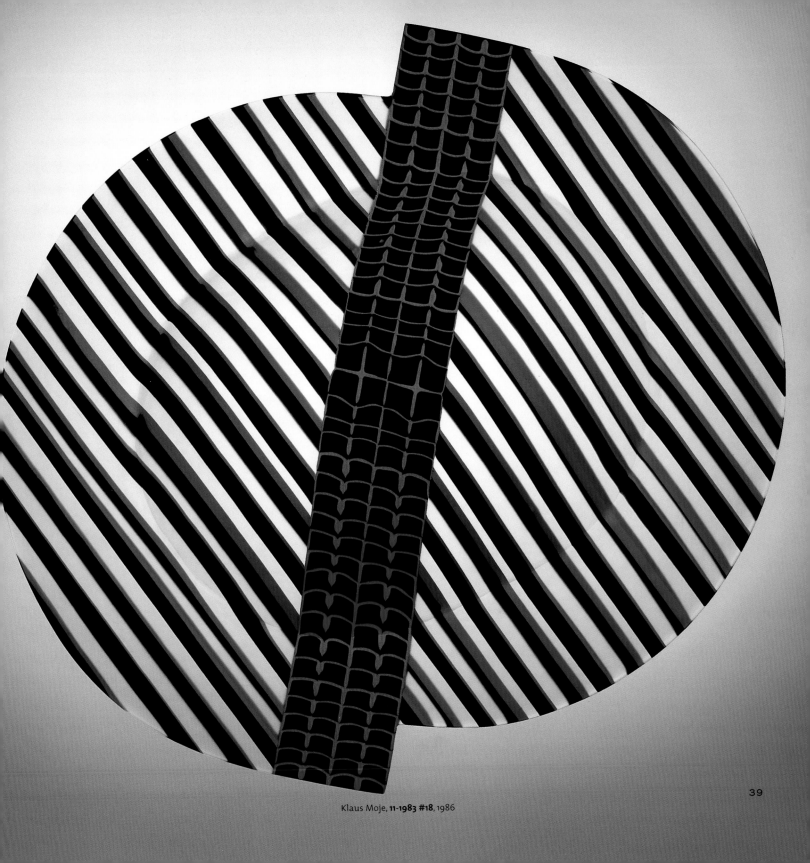

39

Klaus Moje, **11-1983 #18**, 1986

Klaus Moje, **Untitled #48**, 1995

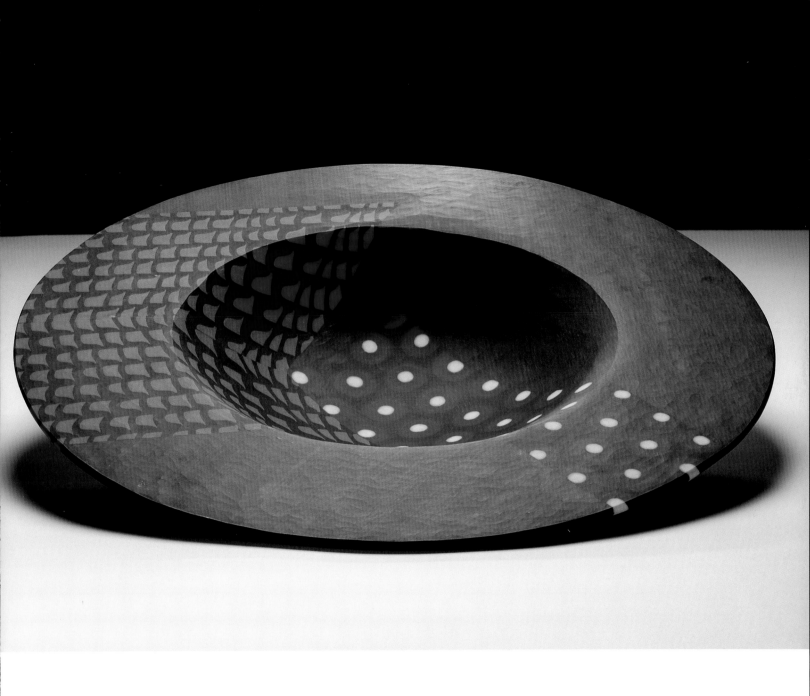

Klaus Moje, **2-1990 #9**, 1990

Klaus Moje, **4-1994 #34**, 1994

Klaus Moje, **7-1990 #31**, 1990

Toots Zynsky, **Scalmana**, 2003

Toots Zynsky, **Chaos in Paradise**, 1995

ORNAMENTATION and embellishment—"the decorative impulse"—have not had an easy go of it in modern art. Apologists for modernist values announced their mission as establishing a new order of truth, of liberating art from the yoke of dogged illustration, narrative, commemoration, and moral uplift. Those quaint values, they asserted, were better fulfilled in photographs or literature or monuments or religion. Art, they reasoned with revolutionary heroism—truly *modern* art—would obey its own laws and explore its own nature. A modern painting need not—indeed, ought not—be obligated to instruct or to persuade with verisimilitude; a painting is pigment in a medium applied to a surface, and therefore that is what it should appear to be. Nothing more, nothing less. The virtue of the artist lay not in rendering images but in revealing the attributes—style, form, technique—of the art itself. Decoration per se served less to reveal style, form, and technique than to obscure these attributes, and in some cases to disguise or distract from their absence. *Modern* art would eschew decoration in favor of truly formal construction. The modern renunciation of the decorative impulse took hold early in the twentieth century. But by the 1970s, with the ascendance of feminist art, the pattern-and-decoration movement in painting, and the rise of the studio glass movement, the decorative impulse had been somewhat rehabilitated in the larger art world, and it no longer provokes potent critical controversy. Decoration, adornment, whimsicality, and even preciousness definitely thrive in contemporary glass art.

Jorge Pardo deliberately blurs the distinction between fine art and decorative art in handsomely designed sculptural objects (and architectural designs) that often have utilitarian purposes. He regards his untitled hand-blown lighting fixtures as illuminated sculptures that also serve to light a space. Pardo has likewise designed objects that are fully functional as furniture as

Jorge Pardo, **Untitled**, 2001

well as an architecture-scale structure intended to serve as a house. The fact that he creates these sculptures and installational works—which anybody would rightly call lamps, tables, and houses—within the context of the visual art world reveals in high relief his strategy of undercutting the imputed distinction between art and design, between decorative and fine art. Pae White likewise positions herself simultaneously and seamlessly in the realms of design and art, again begging the question of where the boundary lies—and whether there really is one. She posits no qualitative creative distinction between the books she designs, the furniture she builds, or the sculptures she makes, and she freely works in whatever medium suits her aim. Her **Gimlet 1–4** is a series of arrangements of blown, mirrored glass bricks displayed directly on the floor. (For this exhibition, White plans to design a site-specific installation of similar glass bricks.)

Richard Marquis is widely acclaimed for his use of murrine, a kind of glass in which sticks or rods of various colors are bundled together to form a design of some intricacy and then heated, fused, and, while still very hot, drawn into thin "canes"—a process in which the design becomes dramatically reduced in size. The cane is then sliced into small cross sections that in turn can be combined into mosaics and fused into a single object. The visual transformations afforded by this laborious and challenging technique lend themselves to elaborate patterning and decoration. Marquis's works, preposterously shaped vessels such as **Marquiscarpa #38** (p. 50), **D'Marquis Teapot Trophy** (p. 51),

Richard Marquis, **Marquiscarpa #38**, 1992

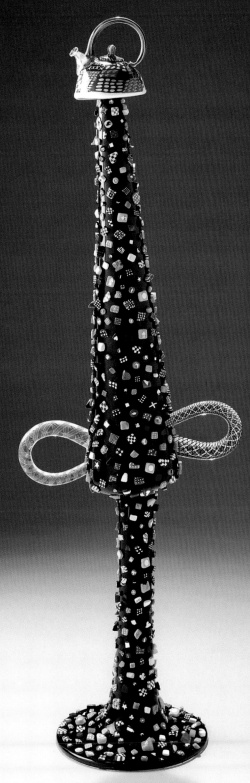

Richard Marquis, **D'Marquis Teapot Trophy**, 1987–88

Richard Marquis, **Goblet Teapot**, 1988

53

Richard Marquis, **American Acid Capsule with Cloth Container**, 1969–70

Richard Marquis, **Teapot**, #21 from the Fabricated Weird series, 1979

or **Goblet Teapot** (p. 52) are, accordingly, always ornately patterned celebrations of their own technique. He revealed his interest in decoration and wit early, in **American Acid Capsule with Cloth Container** (p. 53), a piece reflecting American hippie culture of the 1960s and featuring (presumably) a dose of the psychedelic drug LSD wrapped up in the motif of the Stars and Stripes.

Like Marquis, Flora Mace and her collaborator Joey Kirkpatrick are technical virtuosos. They make oversize blown glass forms in the shapes of fruits, such as **Zanfirico Still Life** (p. 56). *Zanfirico* is a nineteenth-century variation of *filigrana*, originally developed by master craftsmen in Venice in the sixteenth century, using thin glass canes to produce internal bands of intricate lacy patterning; it is the essence of decoration for its own sake and persists in a style that can only be described as timeless.

Whimsicality is the inverse of the rigor that is the hallmark of high modernism. Whim is not the same as play. Play, and the free exercise of the imagination, everyone would agree, are essential elements of a healthy personality; and play can also be purposeful, as in sport or any of the arts. Whimsy, by contrast, suggests caprice and impulse. Yet whimsy is a respected and welcome attribute of much contemporary glass. It undercuts the earnestness of such decorative modes as the baroque, the rococo, and the Victorian, while still demanding technical prowess and skill. Whimsy is therefore somewhat ironic and can be quite sophisticated.

Flora Mace and Joey Kirkpatrick, **Zanfirico Still Life**, 1995

Dan Dailey, **Woman Offering Water to a Porcupine**, 1981

Dan Dailey has long created whimsical figurative art in glass. **Woman Offering Water to a Porcupine** (p. 57) depicts with friezelike formality just what its title indicates. Questions about this unlikely scenario can be asked, but probably cannot be answered. How did this encounter between the woman and the notoriously defensive/aggressive animal come about? Why is she offering the porcupine succor? What is its likely response? That this tableau is reported with utterly deadpan delivery on the circumference of an elegant and boldly proportioned conic vessel of frosted glass renders its humor all the more loopy. **Pompadour**, a portrait of nobody in particular, is a delicious caricature of a suave dandy, smug enough in his debonair mien to crown himself with a silly coiffure. Dailey's whimsicality is rooted in a mock seriousness that is faintly ironic. Hank Murta Adams's **Fernando** (p. 60) is a similarly caricaturish portrait of a wistful, dreamy-looking sort, dominated by an outlandish head of metal hairs. A comparable irony bristles in the cactus-like stalks of Flo Perkins's slyly titled **My Third Arid Dream** (p. 61), which is unabashedly wacky in temper. The cacti's colorful trunks and prickly needles do not conform to those of natural plants but serve as a playful essay in composition and color. And they are slightly heretical within glass practice: the needles are not glass but soft little points of silicone rubber. This is the artist's concession to safety; but for glass purists the work is as mischievous as it is whimsical.

Dan Dailey, **Pompadour**, 2004

Hank Murta Adams, **Fernando**, c. 2001

Flo Perkins, **My Third Arid Dream**, 1981–82

FOR A MEDIUM

that can appear so ethereal that it borders on invisibility, glass can also be among the most physically present materials at an artist's disposal. Daily we encounter glass in its lightest and most fragile forms—a drinking container that breaks if it is dropped, a wine goblet that cracks if it tips over, a windowpane that shatters if it is pressed too firmly when being cleaned. But when artists heat glass until it is molten for casting, they produce some of the densest of objects, so much so that they are often translucent rather than transparent (without the addition of pigment). Such works, even when not particularly large, can have a monumentality about them. Howard Ben Tré works almost exclusively in cast glass, creating stolid forms that look as though they could withstand an earthquake. His **Urn 4** has a visual and physical heft that could not be further from Věra Lišková's delicate glass **Music** or Flo Perkins's prickly **My Third Arid Dream**. Ben Tré, who also makes large-scale works and has handled many public commissions, imbues even his much smaller sculptures with gravitas and aesthetic force. Daniel Clayman's untitled object (p. 65) treads ground somewhere between earthiness and heavy industry, combining a massive flowerlike frosted glass form with a bronze pod that encases it like a seed. Displayed directly on the floor, this massive piece asserts its robust presence within the viewer's customary territory. **Object III** (p. 66) by the Czech artist František Vízner is a luminous midnight-blue cast glass object that looks, in contour, as if it might have been a section cleanly lopped

Howard Ben Tré, **Urn 4**, 1990

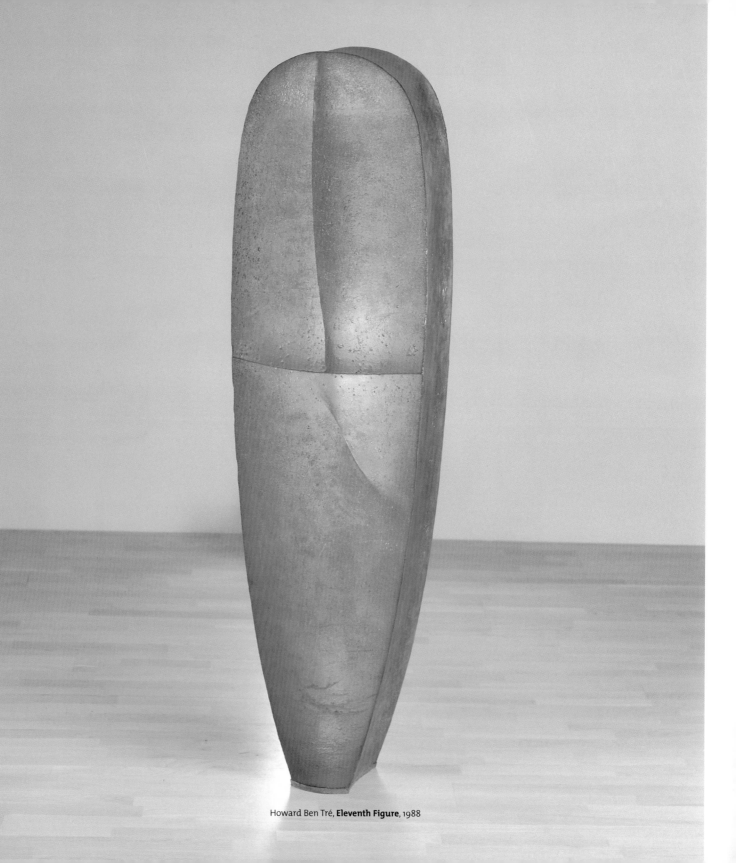

Howard Ben Tré, **Eleventh Figure**, 1988

Daniel Clayman, **Untitled**, 2001

František Vízner, **Object III**, 1989

off the bottom of a large sphere. Its top surface, however, is not flat but divided into two shallow concave depressions bisected by a very slight yet precisely defined edge. The visual power of this strongly composed object results from the manner in which it seems to be pulling itself apart from within. Vízner's fellow Czechs, the husband-and-wife team Stanislav Libenský and Jaroslava Brychtová, make cast glass constructions that can weigh hundreds of pounds and yet glow with a luminosity that suggests, as in Vízner's work, a vital

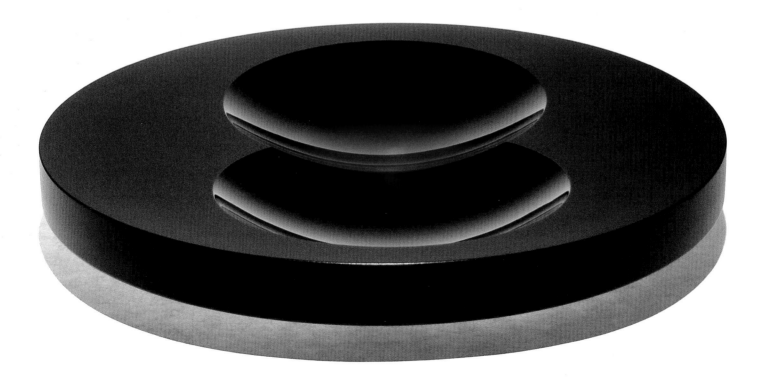

František Vízner, **Bowl**, 1994

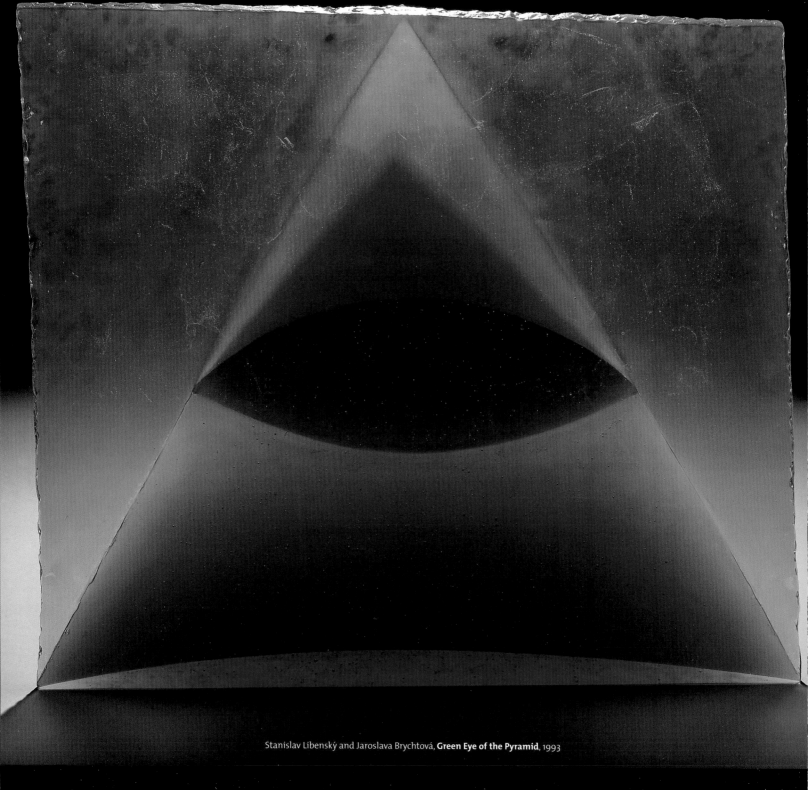

Stanislav Libenský and Jaroslava Brychtová, **Green Eye of the Pyramid**, 1993

internal energy. Their **Green Eye of the Pyramid** evokes the iconic power and entombed mystery of the ancient pyramids, while the eye shape, clearly visible in the pyramid's interior, suggests an omniscient presence at its core.

Though glass is an industrially manufactured product, some glass does come directly from the earth. Indeed, quartz, volcanic obsidian, and fulgurite,

Stanislav Libenský and Jaroslava Brychtová, **Arcus I**, 1990

which is produced by lightning strikes, are three naturally occurring forms of glass. Some glass artists are drawn to this natural quality and deal with the material in ways that emphasize—and sometimes even imitate—its primal aspects. Karla Trinkley works in *pâte de verre*, literally "glass paste," made of ground glass the texture of coarse sand that is placed in a mold and heated until the granules fuse. When the mold is cracked open, the object that emerges looks as if it had been excavated from a primeval burial site. Trinkley's intricately colored forms, such as **El Tajin**, are usually very complex and have a constructed, nearly architectonic quality, but it is their particular materiality that announces their ultimate inspiration not in the studio but in nature. Even more crusty and primeval in appearance is the rugged-looking but very fragile *pâte de verre* vessels (pp. 74–5) by Diane Hobson. Ivan Mareš looks more toward the biosphere for his inspiration, typically creating imposing cast glass works that resemble generative life forms, as in **Nautilus** (p. 76), or **Haystack** (p. 77), which fairly glows from within. That such inorganic, mineral compounds can be made to appear so vital, so biotic, is testimony to both the expressive properties of the medium and the power of Mareš's artistic imagination.

The ovoid form of Jack Wax's **Issue** is dark and enigmatic. Its hundreds of spiky elements may suggest a pinecone, or perhaps the egg case of some insect,

Karla Trinkley, **El Tajin**, 1985

Karla Trinkley, **Tut**, 1984

Diane Hobson, **Vessel**, 1988

Diane Hobson, **Vessel**, c. 1987

Ivan Mareš, **Nautilus**, 1999

or a newborn porcupine, or even a life form from another world. Whatever it is, it looks dangerous and grotesque, and its visual and textural fascination is as palpable as its thorny surface. Less menacing, but equally alluring, are the sand-cast serpentine things that are Lynda Benglis's **MI** (p. 80) and **Emmett** (p. 81). As a feminist artist, Benglis has long used glass in her sculpture. At a time when minimalists—virtually all of them male—were working in rugged industrial materials to produce supremely rational and rectilinear art, Benglis was drawn to glass as a natural and "soft" medium, whose malleability evoked intuitive, organic associations.

Lynda Benglis, **MI**, 1984

Lynda Benglis, **Emmett**, 1993

ANTIQUITY

had many uses for glass, some of them patently spiritual. Naturally occurring specimens of glass, including tektites, the dark, glassy material formed when meteorites heat up in the atmosphere, were treasured for their rarity and regarded as marvels and omens. Primitive mirrors, made of polished volcanic obsidian, were thought to have magical powers. Man-made glass figurines and amulets often played a role in religious rites and rituals. And glass cameos and funerary emblems were especially abundant in ancient Egyptian civilizations. Encyclopedic and anthropological museums throughout the world reveal the impressive range of ancient glass. It is hardly surprising that artists working in glass today would look retrospectively at that tradition, just as painters or sculptors look at their respective traditions. Indeed, many contemporary glass artists pay homage to, and borrow liberally from, examples of ancient glass; and even if their works have an unmistakably contemporary look, their art is assertively rooted in archaism.

Totems, ceremonial masks, and related ritual objects, especially as drawn from extinct or exotic cultures, abound in this direction of recent glass work. William Morris makes sculptures that suggest archaeological finds, such as **Burial Raft** (pp. 84–5) or **Dahl Sheep**, a massive white canopic urn with a lid in the form of a ram's head. Canopic urns were used in ancient Egypt to hold the entrails of embalmed bodies. Whether Morris chooses the form of these vessels strictly as a vehicle for his virtuoso technical skills or, more philosophically, as a memento mori to remind the viewer of the inevitability of death is

William Morris, **Burial Raft**, 1991

Seth Randal, **Fit for a Queen**, 1998

open to question; but it is worth noting that bones, skulls, and other artifacts of death frequently appear in his work, and that the obvious overtures to Egyptian art are likewise overtures to a culture steeped in the mythos of death. Motifs of ancient Egypt exert a similar attraction for Seth Randal, whose **Fit for a Queen** pairs a regal female head with a suitably majestic male head. The dense glass used to depict this royal couple resembles alabaster or translucent stone, and the glow that emanates from them (produced by internal low-wattage lightbulbs) confers a reverential aura to their connubial nobility.

Native American culture is alluded to in Robert Willson's **Ranch Totem** (p. 88), which features a vertical arrangement of what appear to be ears of corn. It is unlikely that a Native American would acknowledge this glass conceit as valid in any indigenous culture, but Willson's creation does evince his interest in totemism, the veneration of animals or natural objects believed to have spiritual significance. Bertil Vallien's **Head** (p. 89) is an effigy of a human head, studded all over with nails. It is a fearsome image, and this unsettling idol possesses the visual and psychological potency of a voodoo doll or evil charm.

While the three-dimensional latticework—a technical tour de force— that defines the structure of Jay Musler's **Karma Coma** (p. 91) may at first glance appear to be thoroughly abstract, a careful second look reveals that its form is an only partially abstracted mask; the traits of a human face can be clearly discerned. Musler's mask, fabricated from smaller pieces of glass, has

Robert Willson, **Ranch Totem**, 1983

Bertil Vallien, **Head**, 1997

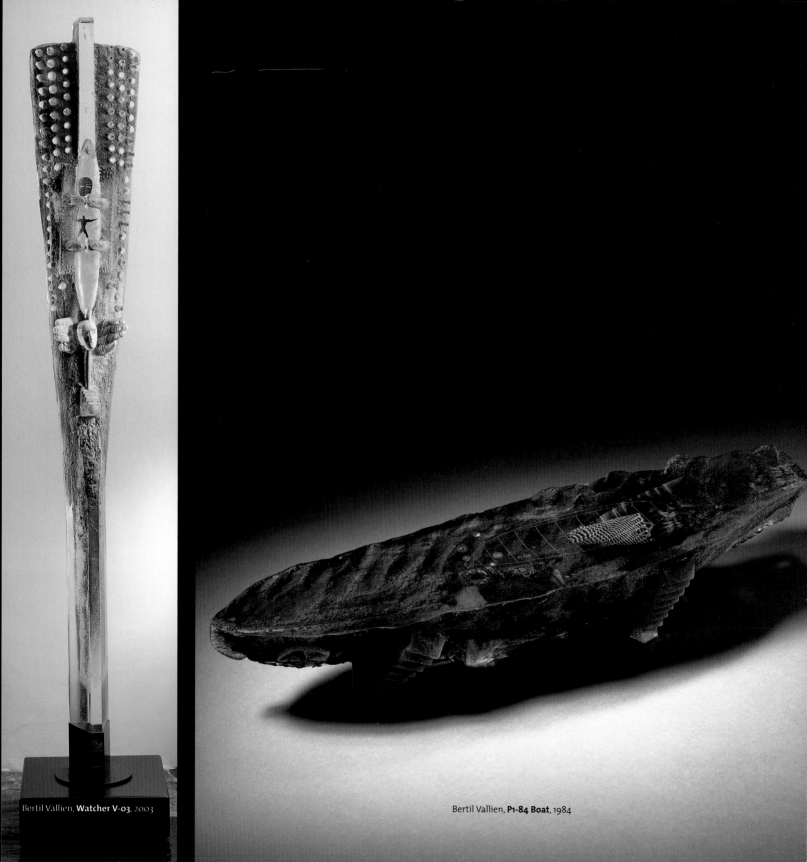

Bertil Vallien, **Watcher V-03**, 2003

Bertil Vallien, **P1-84 Boat**, 1984

Jay Musler, **Karma Coma**, 1999

Jay Musler, **Cityscape**, 1982

Robert Carlson, **Quan-Yin**, 1993

the elongated shape and stylized facial features of many African ritual masks, even as it merges that form with modern geometric abstraction. Robert Carlson's **Quan-Yin** is altogether contemporary in its appearance, but it is a kind of totem pole in its own way, comprising a vertical balancing act of heraldic figures, mythological icons, and exotic patterning based on plant and animal forms, all of these supporting a drinking goblet at the top. Carlson's confabulation of forms is entirely fanciful—not at all to be mistaken for any sanctified ritual vessel from any actual culture—and presents itself as a fantasia of totemic or talismanic motifs.

In Western art, there is a long—and long-contested—tradition of exoticism, in which European and American artists depict distant cultures in idealized and often distorted ways that play up the picturesque and the incompletely understood ethos of alien cultures for aesthetic pleasure and imaginative titillation. There can be no doubt that such practice in contemporary glass begs questions of cultural imperialism, romanticized stereotypes, and misplaced regard for authentic cultural signifiers; but these are apparently not questions posed by the artists themselves—which in turn begs questions of the appropriateness of that critique to the objects at hand. Whether it is sufficient to accept the artists' intentions as the final standard by which their works are to be appreciated must be answered by individual viewers.

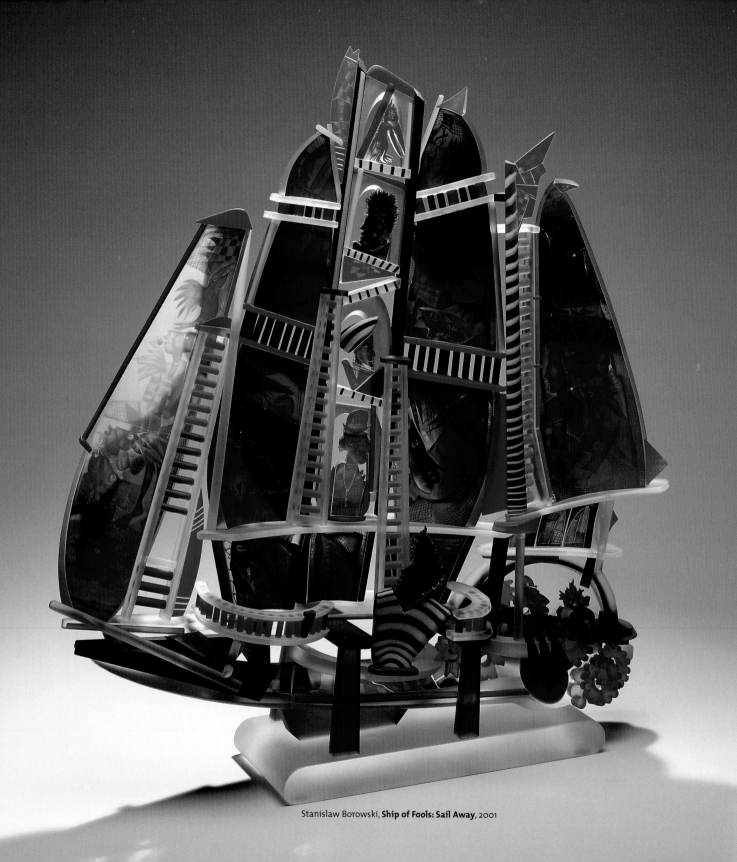

Stanislaw Borowski, **Ship of Fools: Sail Away**, 2001

PERHAPS more than any other medium in the plastic arts, glass has historical and symbolic associations with knowledge, discovery, and perception. Mirrors let us know ourselves, at least physically, as they reflect the world immediately surrounding us and our place and appearance in it. Windows allow us to look out at the public world or to peer into a private world. Reading glasses are a practical necessity for many, and they symbolize studiousness and wisdom. Glass lenses in telescopes and microscopes enable scientists to study the infinite and the infinitesimal. Stained glass windows in cathedrals encourage us to perceive realities beyond the physical universe or to look deeply within. Little wonder that glass exerts considerable appeal to artists whose work is highly conceptual.

Stanislaw Borowski borrows from cultural notions about mythic journeys and perilous ocean voyages to inform his **Ship of Fools: Sail Away**. A colorful and multifaceted work formally, its content is elliptical, implying a narrative without actually presenting one. Rather, it encourages an associative process in which the viewer is free to wonder about the ship's mission, its passengers, and its destiny, in what may be called a proto-narrative strategy. Ginny Ruffner employs the technique of lampworking, or flameworking—manipulating glass rods directly in the flame of a tabletop burner. The decorative, lithe, and colorful fingerlike forms that snake in and around her works are her stylistic signature, though her art is almost always figurative. Often her sources derive from classical mythology, as in **Beauty as Medusa** (p. 96). Medusa, one of the

Ginny Ruffner, **Beauty as Medusa**, 1990

Ginny Ruffner, **Beauty's Alter Ego as a Tornado**, 1990

Ginny Ruffner, **Conceptual Narrative Morphing up the Evolutionary Ladder**, 1998

three Gorgons, had snakes for hair, and was so monstrous that anyone looking at her was turned to stone. The myth is rich in allegorical meanings; Ruffner's Beauty series suggests that beauty itself—particularly decorative beauty—may be excessive, grotesque, and dangerous, a force to be dealt with adroitly.

In Richard Meitner's **Progress IV** (p. 100), a blown and enameled glass sculpture, a human figure with the head of a bird is connected by a glass pipe from his posterior to a Florence flask—a piece of glassware found in every chemical laboratory. Perhaps, in this curious scenario, the bird-man is the distillate of some alchemical process taking place in the flask, the result of some scientific experiment gone awry; or perhaps the flask is the product of the bird-man blowing glass, but from the wrong end. Glass art seems to ridicule science—and itself—in this humoresque.

Ann Wolff likewise employs proto-narrative as the basis of her art; but unlike Borowski or Meitner, she provides provocative clues, like pieces of a puzzle, that the viewer can piece together, at least tentatively, to grope at a possible intended meaning. **Outside the Kitchen** (p. 102) uses sheet glass almost like a slate to present the elements of a story. The upper part of the glass panel shows rudimentary images of a nude man and woman, joined together by bands—possibly ribbons of matrimony or of dependence—which are being cut by scissors that are operated by an unseen hand. The couple is surrounded by a picture of a child and other images of domestic life. The

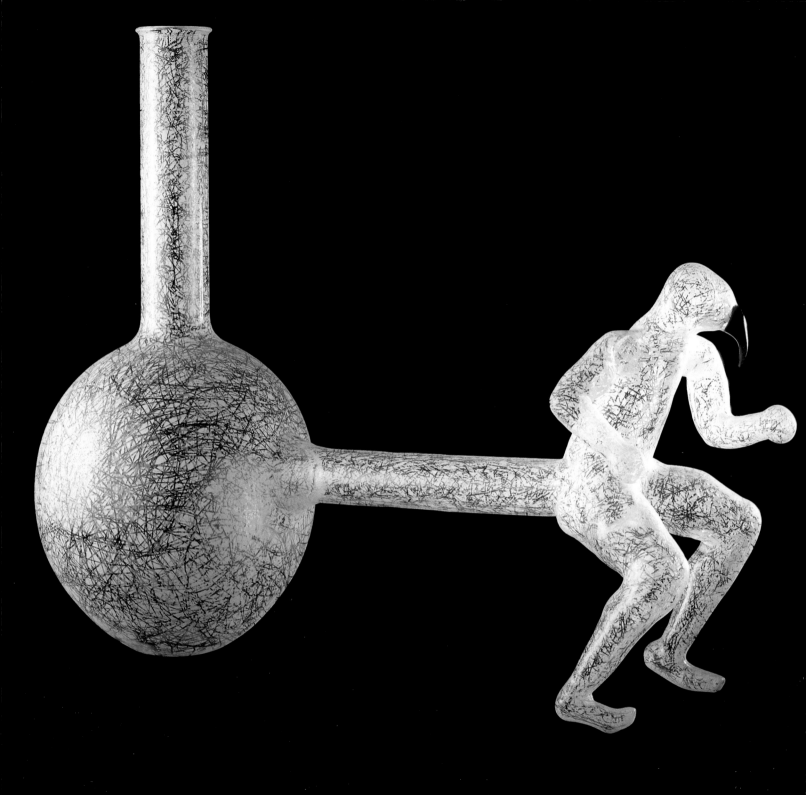

Richard Meitner, **Progress IV**, 1998

Richard Meitner, **Branch**, 2001

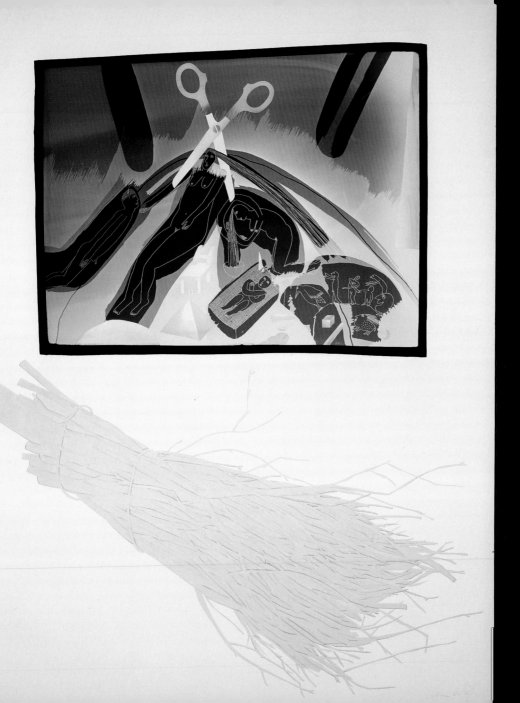

tableau suggests a family life disrupted, though the reasons are vague and hard to pinpoint, as is often the case when families break up. Below this framed tableau, and acid-etched into its undersurface, is the ghostly image of a broom. Deployed almost as if it were a caption, the broom suggests the desire for erasure, or riddance, or a clean sweep of the memory of it all.

The brothers Einar and Jamex de la Torre incorporate an eclectic mix of materials ranging from bottle caps to dominoes to video in their constructions, but they often feature glass as the primary material. Their emphatic eclecticism reflects an impulse to synthesize, to bring together disparate elements into a complicated mélange or, as they would describe it, a menudo of many ingredients. The brothers were born in Mexico, raised in Dana Point, a beach community in Southern California, and now live and work on both sides of the international border that separates San Diego County from the state of Baja California. Their work always entails bicultural critique with a political edge, as reflected in the busy title of their elaborate wall piece: **Narcochic (celebrating the nouveau-rich aesthetic of the narco-drug traffickers in Mexico and Miami)** (p. 104). The work is in the form of a sunburst that radiates from an ancient Aztec sun god whose crown is inscribed "Miami." Their ribald humor also animates **Alchemy** (p. 105), a small shrine, flanked on either side by bottles of "poisonous" beer, a testimony to the potential surprises inherent in all kinds of chemical transmutations.

Einar and Jamex de la Torre, **Narcochic (celebrating the nouveau-rich aesthetic of the narco-drug traffickers in Mexico and Miami)**, 2003

Einar and Jamex de la Torre, **Alchemy**, 1996

Silvia Levenson's art is also politically edgy, though with a more biting irony. Her translucent **Pink Cinderella**, made of cast glass, certainly evokes the glass slipper bestowed upon the fabled maiden to win the hand of Prince Charming. Watched over by a fairy godmother and rescued from a bleak life of subjugation to her abusive stepsisters, Cinderella would seem to embody the iconic hope of womanly liberation from a life of dreary domestic serfdom. But Levenson's glass slippers come with a twist: inside each shoe, sticking upward into the would-be wearer's heel, is a sharp tack. Levenson punctures the Cinderella myth with her indirect reminder that the popular Disney version, familiar to just about everyone, casts women either as aggressively abusive ogres or as powerless waifs dependent on supernatural help and masculine rescue—culminating in marriage—if they are to be saved. In such a vision, the Cinderella story is as much a trap as a life of drudgery and servitude.

Judith Schaechter is among a sizable number of artists working today in stained glass. Though this art form has been usually rooted in religious themes and confined to church windows, Schaechter's stained glass tableaux are usually freestanding and decidedly not religious in tone. However, they often are psychologically and morally freighted. Her **Dreams of the Fisherman's Wife** (p. 109) is an enigmatic vignette. This triptych depicts a scantily clad, dispirited woman stepping from the ocean in the background onto the seashore. Flanking the edges of the tableau are two menacing octopi, sitting atop the waves. Did they rescue the woman at sea and return her to land?

Silvia Levenson, **Pink Cinderella**, 2000

Silvia Levenson, **Sogni Sospesi (Suspended Dreams)** from the Trans-Ferirsi series, 1995

Judith Schaechter, **Dreams of the Fisherman's Wife**, 2004

Was she perhaps their prisoner? Are they coming to pursue her now? No one can say.

Brussels-based Wim Delvoye is best known for his grand mechanical systems that replicate, with precision machinery and chemical processes, what the human digestive system accomplishes quite naturally. In fact, Delvoye is preoccupied with the human body and its intersections with modern-day technology. Adapting the latest imaging techniques from medicine and new printing techniques from digital photography, Delvoye has made several series of stained glass windows. The Chapel series incorporates X-ray images of the internal systems of the human body and also of people engaged in various activities, including sexual ones. His contemporary look at these eternally compelling subjects matches the visual and imaginative attraction of any church window from the Gothic period.

Since the AIDS epidemic began in the 1980s, there has been a renewed interest in the body as subject among many American and European artists. As demonstrated in Delvoye's art, this interest is not necessarily the traditional one of idealizing or aestheticizing the body—as in a painted nude by Nicolas Poussin or a bronze nude by Gaston Lachaise—but a more clinical fixation on the human animal, with all that can befall it. In his **Eye Bath** (p. 112) and **Mortar and Pestle** (p. 113) Tony Cragg does not directly portray the body or its attributes. Yet the medicinal references to disease and cure, embodied

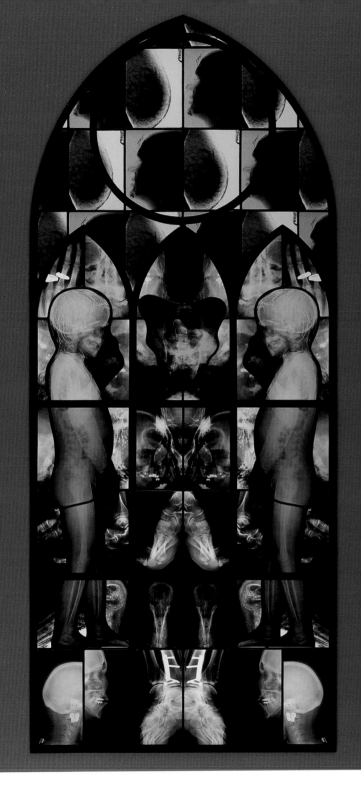

Wim Delvoye, **March**, from the Chapel series, 2001

Wim Delvoye, **September**, from the Chapel series, 2001

Tony Cragg, **Eye Bath**, 1986

113

Tony Cragg, **Mortar and Pestle**, 1986

Michael Aschenbrenner, **Graduation Gowns Lay in Rags at Their Feet**, from the Damaged Bone series, 1980–86

in the outsize renditions of clinical and laboratory equipment, remind viewers of, as Hamlet put it, "the thousand natural shocks that flesh is heir to."

Michael Aschenbrenner was an American combat soldier in Vietnam in the 1960s, where, in an accidental explosion of munitions, he suffered severe injuries to his legs. As he was medevacked out and hoisted into the helicopter, a heavy barrage of enemy fire was trained on him. Miraculously, he survived both the explosion and the bullets, but he required multiple surgeries and many months of healing and physical therapy to regain the use of his legs. He later went to art school and learned how to work in glass. But his youthful near-loss of life was as emotionally debilitating and scarring as it was physically, and for a six-year period, from 1980 to 1986, he became obsessed with making glass sculptures of human bones. He produced thousands of them, all in richly colored cast glass, each wrapped with bandages or rags tied to makeshift splints of twigs and wires. The Damaged Bone series is a gruesome yet lyrical opus that testifies by its own existence to the persistence of life against catastrophic ruin.

Clifford Rainey's cast glass torsos do recall the idealized torsos of classical sculpture, but in his art they are manipulated by externally imposed conditions, so that they are less subject than object. In **Hollow Torso, No Step Is Final** (p. 116), for example, life-size torsos are set upon low platforms that look like four-legged stools, imparting a sense that they could walk if they desired. They are, however, constrained by circumstance: one form is studded with spikes (like the head by Bertil Vallien), and the other is crimped by C-clamps

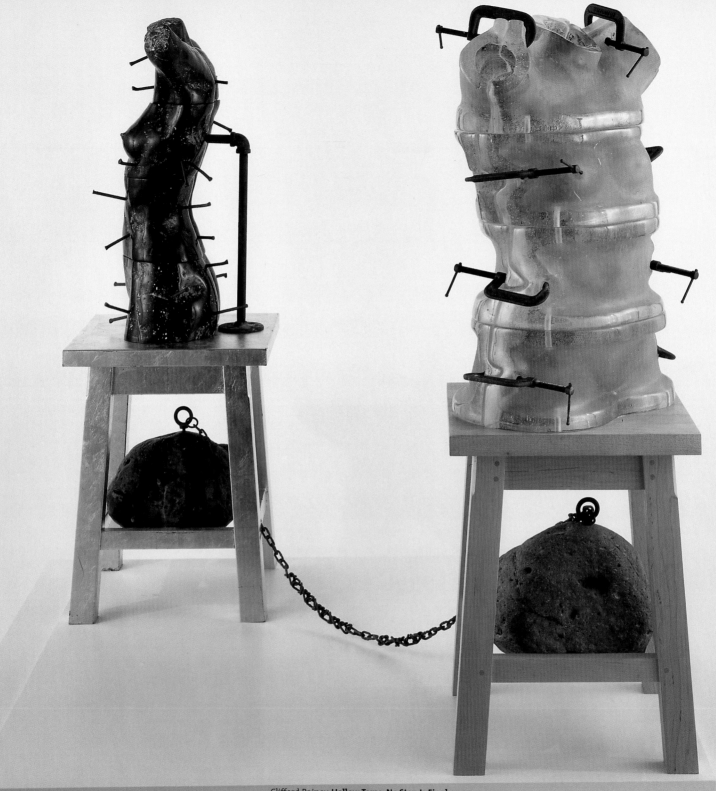

Clifford Rainey, **Hollow Torso, No Step Is Final**, 2000–1

Clifford Rainey, **Caryatid**, 2003

Kiki Smith, **Shed**, 1996

running up and down the flanks, chest, and shoulders. Further impeding them are the heavy rocks borne by their respective platforms and chained to each other. In this psychodrama in glass, the individual figures are literally stuck, mutually dependent and incapable of escape. Rainey's **Caryatid** (p. 117) portrays a related conundrum: a negative (hollow) female torso is entombed in a solid cast glass bottle, like a fly in amber; a corresponding positive torso is liberated from the bottle yet still somewhat constrained in a form that echoes the bottle. Rainey returns to the theme of thralldom again and again in his art; it is the flip side of the theme announced in Ann Wolff's work.

Kiki Smith has long investigated the human body in her sculptures in all mediums, and glass figures prominently in her oeuvre. Bodily fluids are a frequent subject. She has used clear cast glass to represent teardrops and, in **Shed**, rich red opaque glass to represent more than forty drops of blood, each from two to ten inches tall, arrayed in an arc. Every aspect of corporeality appears in her art, and she faces her subject unflinchingly. But in **Tombs** (p. 120), a somewhat anomalous piece for her, there is no artistic representation of a human body or any part of it. The work consists of two shelves supporting sheets of mirrored glass. The only imagery involved, one expects, would be the reflection of the viewer. In fact, because the glass surfaces are quite irregular and wobbly, the viewer's face never appears. The effect of looking into what is known to be a mirror and not seeing oneself can be a disconcerting reminder of one's mortality, which is not only an aspect of corporeality, it is the one ineluctable, certain result of it—perhaps even its primary purpose.

Kiki Smith, **Tombs**, 1989

ARTISTS whose subjects embrace archaic and exotic cultures, narrative, psychological, and political content, and ruminations on the body are all conceptually oriented. That is not to say necessarily that they are "conceptual artists." But some artists working in glass do come out of a conceptual art background and turn to glass much as they might choose any other medium appropriate to their task. The nascent stages of conceptual art in the early 1970s, before there was an acknowledged terminology to denote it, tended to assert a focus on language and ideas as the primary content of a work of art, according these a primacy that surpassed its physical attributes, such as style, form, or technique, and even its very materiality. Early conceptual artists were interested in the way in which the human intelligence orders the world, conscripting inert objects and ascribing meaning to them. It was the thought process itself that was of fundamental import to these artists. Much early conceptual art existed only as written or spoken words, as tables of information, or as performed actions. Over the three decades since its incipient manifestations, conceptual art has itself developed in myriad directions, some of them very physical, and its underlying interests have had a profound influence on a vast range of artists who work in many mediums, including glass.

Rita McBride is not a glass artist per se; she often engages other materials, some of them, like duct tape or plastic wrap, a little off-diet even in the omnivorous world of contemporary sculpture. Yet she always chooses materials appropriate to her aims, and glass is something to which she has returned

Rita McBride, **Chair**, 1997

again and again. Her bentwood-style **Chair**, fashioned from amber murano glass, lacks a seat and is held together by plastic wrap rather than proper screws and brackets. It is very insubstantial for its purported use, more like the outline of a chair. Moreover, precisely because it is a diagram, a three-dimensional limning of a utile object, we perceive it as a representation rather than as the real thing. And yet, precisely because this chair-shaped object is made of glass, it is intensely physical and materially quite real. Typically for McBride, in this piece she confounds what is real and what is concept. Using the medium of glass for its transparency is altogether appropriate to her aim.

Therman Statom has spent much of his artistic life making glass sculptures of three favored subjects: chairs, ladders, and houses. As with McBride's objects, Statom's have no practical purpose, even though they approximate the forms of commonplace things; and like McBride, Statom pretty much eschews studio glass techniques, opting instead to construct his works like a model maker. Generally he cuts forms directly out of sheet glass and then pieces them together with various glues, so that they become rough templates of the objects they represent. Sometimes, however, they become containers, as when Statom fills them with pounds and pounds of crushed or shattered plate glass "gravel." He almost always treats the exterior surfaces with applications of gestural oil painting and/or the application of shards of colored glass and other small found objects. He thus is simultaneously a

Therman Statom, **Rey de Sol Mexico**, 1988

sculptor, a painter, an assemblage artist, and a collagist working primarily in glass. The thin glass panes he uses are inherently breakable; and any such chair, ladder, or house (pp. 124–5)—all things that normally provide comfort, safety, support, and general domestic aid in service to daily human needs— would supply only dysfunctional, potentially dangerous assistance. And the sundry bits of paint, broken glass, and trinkets he affixes to their exteriors are like oddments from other moments of creativity, somehow fragmented and gone astray. There is a faint melancholy to Statom's art, as if it represents the obstacles to artistic, or personal, wholeness and completion.

Sherrie Levine addresses a different sort of challenge to artists: the need—or lack of need—to be original. Since the Renaissance, Western civilization has placed a premium on artistic genius, which is usually defined not only by technical and formal accomplishment but by originality as well. The great artist not only must be imaginative and technically talented but must be an innovator whose achievements are unmistakably his or her own. We may grant followers and acolytes their due respect, but it is to original artistic genius that we pay greatest homage. Levine adroitly precipitated an often fractious discourse in the 1970s when she decided to "appropriate" art historical precedents as the basis of her own practice. Among her early exploits: she photographed reproductions of revered modern masterworks in standard textbooks and then displayed the photographic prints as her art; for another project, she purchased Library of Congress prints of WPA-era photographs by

Walker Evans, made from second-generation negatives, then rephotographed the prints herself, and then printed and exhibited the resulting photographs— now several generations removed from the originals. Her attempt was not at all to fool anybody; indeed, she relied upon common knowledge of the true identity of her sources as the strategy to catalyze a critique of the very notions of originality and authenticity. Her glass **Crystal Newborn** (p. 128) and **Black Newborn** (p. 129) are authorized casts of Constantin Brancusi's 1915 marble sculpture **Newborn** in the collection of the Philadelphia Museum of Art. Substituting glass, which had so little place in modern art, for marble extended her critique to issues of materiality as well.

Josiah McElheny also plumbs the history of art—glass art in particular— in his conceptual investigations. He brings extraordinary technical and imaginative capacities to the medium, and he employs these skills to dazzling effect, creating works in the manner of almost every period or culture. His **Ornament and Crime** (p. 130) is an enclosed glass cabinet containing a collection of the most exquisitely formed, virtually perfect, blown glass vessels, of every generic shape: cones, cylinders, spheres, ovals. Within their cabinet they are presented as specimens literally under glass. Moreover, all are fabricated in the same ashen-white glass, which gives them a unifying ghostly quality. These objects are like ur-forms, seeming to exist outside of time and in their own space. This curious exhibit is accompanied by a passage of text, displayed nearby, from *Ornament and Crime* by Adolf Loos, the Austrian modernist

Sherrie Levine, **Crystal Newborn**, 1993

Sherrie Levine, **Black Newborn**, 1994

Josiah McElheny, **Ornament and Crime**, 2001–2

architect and critic. Loos argued truculently in his 1908 tract that ornamentation and decoration were false values in architecture and design. A rationalist, he held that austerity of form was necessary for design integrity and honesty. He went so far as to call ornamentation, including applied color, a crime—an aesthetic crime, albeit one with intellectual and ethical import. In his homage to Loos, McElheny has fashioned his glass vessels in the austere manner Loos called for, something rare within the richly decorative history of glass. But it is an ironic homage because, as McElheny's work demonstrates, Loos's vaunted austerity is simply a conceit, another fashion with no more—or less—validity than any other style. McElheny's own reined-in elegance is, in essence, another type of ornamentation, as unnatural and deliberate as the most Victorian of decorative patterns, gewgaws, and gingerbread. Just to punctuate the point, McElheny bedecks his dour glass cabinet with two lamps, each sporting as a shade the cutest little ruffled cloth skirt you ever saw. These shades are akin to those Loos would have known in turn-of-the-century Vienna, coexisting with the stringent design reforms he proposed.

Jill Reynolds's conceptual investigations take a different direction, into the realm of science. Her art is centered on ethical issues surrounding contemporary biological research and biotechnology. **Replicate** (pp. 132–3) presents two nearly identical humanoid glass forms—humanoid, not human, because while they possess arms, legs, a torso, and heads, they also have four fingers on each hand and antennae. They are either mutant humans or alien

Jill Reynolds, **Replicate**, 2003

life forms. In any case, they are grotesque, creepy figures, attached to each other by a rubber tube, like a symbiotic lifeline that joins their destinies. Yet there are subtle discrepancies between them, perhaps such natural variations as differentiate even identical twins, or perhaps evidence of a botched cloning, in which the replicant turns out to have fatal flaws or potentially monstrous deformities. **Replicate** is Reynolds's cautionary tale about engineered biotic forms.

GLASS HAS A LONG historical association with science and, before the development of scientific method, with alchemy and the transformation of base materials into pure and valued ones. Alchemy is popularly spoken of as if it were dedicated to refining dross into gold with the aim of enriching fortunes. But alchemy was the physical science of its time, an attempt to understand the makeup of the created universe and the laws that governed it. Michael Glancy would not be properly described as a conceptual artist, but his intricately materialist art is centered in scientific and philosophical concepts, as evinced by references in the titles of his works to biology, molecular physics, astronomical bodies, relativity, mathematics, and infinitude. The works themselves incorporate blown and plate glass, brass, copper, bronze, silver, and gold, and on occasion stone, such as black granite. He fuses these materials in a process known as electroforming, in which a high-voltage charge is

Michael Glancy, **Molecular TGE**, 1984

Michael Glancy, **Incognito Ruby Guardian**, 1988

Michael Glancy, **UV Expansion**, 1994

Michael Glancy, **Infinite Obsessions**, 1999

Michael Glancy, **Biomorphic Ganglia**, 2003

passed through them. The strongly transformative process, together with his scientific interests, seems to position his creations within the practice of alchemy—at the intersection of physics and metaphysics—as much as in the domain of art. The forms he creates possess an ineffable, cosmic aura. Characteristically in his work, a geometric volume—a globe, cylinder, or ovoid—sits atop a plane. In **Molecular TGE** (p. 135), an optically pure blown glass sphere, clad in copper and silver with many protruding windows or portals, rests on a flat surface of glass variegated with metallic channels. This arrangement, in turn, sits atop another glass plate scored with many sunken small circular forms linked by a network of straight grooves. In this abstract composition, the self-contained geometric solid dominates the "landscape" that expands laterally beneath it. There is no activity clearly described or alluded to, and yet the forms suggest a sense of centered authority poised to act on, or to impose its agency upon, an indefinite vastness. In the poetry of Glancy's art there is always the impression of a momentous cosmological event or potential, perhaps the moment before the Creation or the Big Bang.

Bruce Nauman has been a pioneering conceptual, installation, video, and performance artist who recognizes the underlying function of language in all human perception and ideation. Many of his works involve text in the form of a list of words or word combinations or phrases, and he often displays these texts as neon signs mounted directly on a wall or the side of a building.

Bruce Nauman, **Human Nature / Life Death / Knows Doesn't Know**, 1983

Glass, of course, is integral to a neon sign, for it is only through the transparency and malleability and subsequent stability of glass that the glowing neon gas can be shaped as intended. Neon signs are ordinarily used for advertising or to identify spaces in the public landscape. They are an aspect of popular culture and part of our visual vernacular. When Nauman began using neon in the late 1960s, he chose it specifically because it was not associated with fine art, and because his illuminated words made no particular sense as advertising. His choice served to create an alien work that required a new kind of attention from the audience. Nauman's **Human Nature / Life Death / Knows Doesn't Know** (p. 141) is among his most important neon works. The intermittently flashing words around its circular perimeter—life, death; love, hate; pleasure, pain—and the phrases crisscrossing its diameter—knows, doesn't know; cares, doesn't care; matters, doesn't matter; animal nature, human nature, human animal—are ingredients of every human personality, and in various mixtures define each individual. Each of us knows and doesn't know certain things; cares or doesn't care about certain people, ideas, or parts of life; and so on. Nauman's blinking neons add up to a kind of existential meditation on the nature of human existence, all of whose possibilities and failures are contained within its rubrics. His glowing words may be truly described as the secular equivalent of a stained glass cathedral window.

THOUGH GLASS WAS of little interest to modern sculptors, it was of surpassing interest to modern architects, especially of the International Style, such as Ludwig Mies van der Rohe, who exploited its transparency, lightness, sheerness, and overt industrial fabrication to design masterworks of residential, commercial, and civic architecture. But, until recently, architects tended to use glass in the most straightforward way—undisguised, clear, and in sheets applied as cladding, like a skin, or set into openings in steel and concrete structures.

For most architects working in the International Style during the mid-to-late twentieth century, glass was as fundamental as steel in forming buildings that ranged from great skyscrapers to intimate residences. Generally glass was used as a curtain, a sheer exterior that proffered to those on the inside panoramic vistas of the outside world. Tinted glass, occluding views from the outside in, served to protect the privacy of workers or residents. Today glass continues to play a major role in contemporary architecture, but architects and their consulting engineers have found ways to use it with a greater sense of freedom, play, and symbolism.

Having been catalytic in establishing the studio glass movement that stressed the unique handmade object, Dale Chihuly began to think beyond the intimate, making multipart arrangements of glass forms that at first began to modestly creep into space, and then to sprawl, and then positively

Dale Chihuly, **Fiori di Como** (Bellagio Hotel, Las Vegas), 1998

to swell into architecturally scaled tours de force. Occasionally working at imposing sites such as the Citadel in Jerusalem, Lismore Castle in Ireland, or the Beaux Arts–style Union Station in Tacoma, Washington, Chihuly characteristically stages a radiant explosion of color and a profusion of multifaceted organic forms—flames, flowers, leaves, gourds, shells—that are dramatic visual foils to their settings. Perhaps his most self-consciously spectacular project is **Fiori di Como** (pp. 144–5), the eye-popping, jaw-dropping ceiling for the lobby of the Bellagio Hotel in Las Vegas. Flamboyantly dominating a public space of some twenty-one hundred square feet, the work consists of more than two thousand burgeoning floral forms in highly saturated reds, yellows, blues, and everything in between, all suffused with the light that spills down into the room. The effect is exhilarating.

James Carpenter, of James Carpenter Design Associates, describes his primary focus as the transmission, reflection, and refraction of glass in architecture and large-scale sculpture. His **Lens Ceiling** (p. 148), completed in 2000, is a work of public art within the United States Courthouse and Federal Building designed by Richard Meier & Partners in Phoenix, Arizona. The **Lens Ceiling** is, as its name indicates, the actual ceiling of a transparent glass, six-story cylindrical special-proceeding courtroom that stands like a vast drum in the center of the building. The frosted glass ceiling is a spherical segment suspended above the court, transmitting diffused daylight down into the chamber and flooding it with a soft glow. A glass courtroom bathed in the light of day is an apt metaphor for the American concept of justice as a transparent proceeding, open to civic scrutiny and accountable to all.

Ingalill Wahlroos-Ritter, working with the architectural firm Smith-Miller + Hawkinson, was project architect for the 2001 renovation and addition to the **Corning Museum of Glass**, in Corning, New York, the largest such museum in the world. The project included a renovation of the original 1951 Wallace Harrison building and the Steuben glassblowing facility, the refurbishment of the permanent collection galleries, a new entry pavilion, and a theater for educational programs (p. 149). Of course, glass is the featured material of the project, notably the vast expanses of custom-fabricated frameless plates. These are joined with drilled fittings that minimize the hardware and emphasize transparency. The stainless-steel structural supports on either side of the vast panes appear to pass through the glass—a formal innovation that visually blurs the distinction between interior and exterior and, at a subliminal level, imparts a prismatic effect to the entire building. It is a very apt look for a museum of glass.

Eric Owen Moss Architects is based in an industrial district of Culver City, a small city surrounded entirely by the sprawl of greater Los Angeles. Quite a few of Moss's most experimental projects have been constructed locally in existing buildings, all owned by a single developer. The most distinctive directions in Moss's practice lie less in projects built from the ground up than in transformations of existing architecture—much of it otherwise nondescript. Glass is a favored medium, in part because it possesses almost limitless malleability, which appeals to Moss's aesthetics of unbridled shape-shifting.

James Carpenter, **Lens Ceiling** (Phoenix Federal Building), 2000

149

Smith-Miller + Hawkinson, **Corning Museum of Glass renovation** (Corning, NY), 2001

His **Umbrella** (p. 152) is an undulating form made of heat-slumped laminated plate glass. It appears to flounce wildly, like laundry on a clothesline thrashing in a brisk wind, as it erupts from the corner of a boxy structure. Oddly, this canopy shields no entry or other architectural feature; it simply is there. Accessed by a staircase from within the building, the canopy can be utilized as a belvedere, an observation deck from which to view neighboring industrial buildings, some featuring other Moss interventions. But mostly it exists in its own right, a pure architectural form in service to no particular function, save for its own being.

One of the most controversial of recent buildings is **30 St. Mary Axe** (p. 153), designed for the Swiss Re insurance company by Sir Norman Foster of Foster and Partners. Popularly called "the Gherkin," this unusually shaped building resembles less a pickle than a torpedo or a dirigible standing on end. The Gherkin rises forty stories in the heart of London's financial district, handily asserting itself as the dominant feature in the local landscape. Its surface is a latticework of glass triangles and rhomboids that form a spiraling design visible across the city. Surprisingly, while the contour of the building itself appears everywhere curved, each pane of glass in its mosaic surface is flat, with the exception of a single glass cap at the very top. Nonetheless, the tower reads as a buoyant, ballooning presence among some of the stodgiest and straitjacketed office buildings thrown up in the Western world. The glint of the glass, as well as the engineering involved, engenders that formal liveliness. The building won the prestigious Stirling Award for architectural excellence in 2004.

Just across the Thames, the **London Bridge Tower** by Renzo Piano &
Building Workshop (p. 154), some seventy stories and more than a thousand
feet high, will be the tallest building in Europe when it is completed in 2009.
The mixed-use building will include offices, shops, residences, a luxury hotel,
and public piazzas, or viewing galleries, at midlevel and at the uppermost
story. Its piercing slender form has prompted some to describe the planned
structure as a "shard of glass"—no doubt a negative criticism. Piano, however,
describes it as "a vertical town" that, at its pinnacle, disappears into the air.
Piano chose glass for its apparent lightness, its gleam and reflectivity, to lend
an ethereal quality to what will be in fact one of the most massive structures
in Europe.

The **Seattle Public Library** (pp. 156–7), designed by Rem Koolhaas of OMA
(Office for Metropolitan Architecture), is a huge glass sculpture twisting and
torquing like a series of irregularly stacked slabs of space. The internal structure is a continuous ramp that spirals through these rectangular spaces,
enabling visitors to meander through the library stacks. The glass façade
reveals the collection to the outside world—and of course maximizes the
suffusion of daylight for the benefit of readers and workers—while the
extensive interior use of glass serves the same notion of transparency, suggest-
ing that the knowledge and wisdom contained in the library's books are avail-
able to all.

Sir Norman Foster (Foster and Partners), **30 St. Mary Axe** (London), 2004

153

Renzo Piano & Building Workshop, architect's rendering of **London Bridge Tower**, work in progress

In 2004, London-based Zaha Hadid submitted a quite startling proposal for an envisioned **2012 Olympic Village** for New York City (p. 158). In her design some fourteen curvaceous see-through glass towers and three glass pavilions appear to hover just above their parklike setting along the shoreline of Hunters Point in Queens, across the East River from Manhattan. The most notable aspect of these imagined buildings is that they are completely transparent and seem to have no internal skeletons to support their bubblelike forms. It is not evident visually how these structures would be anchored to the ground. All that is certain is that Hadid sees her buildings, her village, as made of glass. It is not at all unusual for architects to propose conceptual or visionary projects as an integral—indeed as a vital—function of their practice. Architects are forever imagining and designing projects that never get built, and architectural competitions by definition are composed mostly of proposals that will not be realized. Nonetheless, Hadid's gesture has conceptual integrity, even though destined to remain only an idea. What is significant is that she has proposed a massive complex—a village of skyscrapers— inspired by a notion of glass as gossamer thin, utterly transparent, virtually dematerialized. Hers is a village in which people of every nation, every race and ethnicity, and every religion come together to live, however briefly, completely in the open, in a space of total visibility. Her glass world is a utopian place, like an Edenic realm before humankind perceived itself to be naked, ashamed, and mistrustful.

Rem Koolhaas (OMA), **Seattle Public Library**, 2004

Zaha Hadid Architects, architect's rendering of proposed **2012 NYC Olympic Village**, 2004

THE GLASS ARTISTS

—sculptors, conceptualists, installation and decorative artists, and architects—in this exhibition cover an expansive field of interests, aesthetics, techniques, and forms. The works present not only strong contrasts, but sometimes even antithetical reasons for being. Yet all of these artists share a deep and abiding fascination with glass, and all have specifically chosen to engage the considerable technical challenges, and range of formal possibilities, that this protean medium offers. Glass: material matters.

ACKNOWLEDGMENTS

All exhibitions have an interesting birth; this one surely has had the longest gestation. Discussions regarding an exhibition of contemporary glass between the Los Angeles County Museum of Art and collectors Daniel Greenberg and his wife, Susan Steinhauser, who helped assemble LACMA's contemporary glass holdings, began as far back as 1991. Through the years this exhibition abided as a highly desirable project, but its actual organization remained elusive through the comings and goings of several curators, department chairs, and museum directors. In the recent past, senior curator Stephanie Barron and Wendy Kaplan, curator and head of the decorative arts department, ensured the continued well-being of this project, and we thank them especially. We also thank LACMA decorative arts curator Thomas Michie for his friendly encouragement and moral support.

When the show ultimately did get under way in earnest, many people deployed their specialized talents at LACMA to produce it. Bruce Robertson, deputy director for exhibitions; Irene Martín, assistant director of exhibition programs; financial analyst Beverley Sabo; and exhibition programs coordinator Janelle Aieta attended to the myriad concerns suggested by their titles.

Moving works of art is always a painstaking process, and moving fragile glass works presents an even greater challenge. Associate registrar Sandy Davis and registrarial assistant Robyn Sanford shared the multifaceted tasks of coordinating the loan requests and the packing, shipping, and inspection of all the works en route to and from the museum. Objects conservator John Hirx and assistant conservator Natasha Cochran were on hand to oversee the safety and welfare of the many objects at all times while they were at LACMA or in transit.

The ever-ready, willing, and able Jeffrey Haskin, manager of art preparation and installation, and his crew expertly installed the delicate works with great care and ingenuity in an exhibition space that was elegantly designed by Bernard Kester and constructed under the supervision of Bill Stahl. Electrician Roosevelt Simpson brought his customary flair for lighting to make the works look their very best. We extend our gratitude to all those who participated in the gallery presentation.

This catalogue is an integral part of the exhibition. We thank photographic services supervisor Peter Brenner and photographer Steven Oliver for their artful picture making, which appears so often in this volume. Cheryle Robertson, coordinator of rights and reproductions, and her assistant Piper Severance did their sleuthing to acquire additional photography and make sure that we had the necessary permissions to feature these pictures as well. Stephanie Emerson, former director of publications, was instrumental in the realization of this volume and making sure that it was adequately nourished. Inspired by the glass art in this show, associate director of graphics Amy McFarland enlivened this volume with its bold and handsome design.

Editor Thomas Frick—always thoughtful, vigilant, and witty—adroitly managed to represent the interests of both the author and the readers of this book. Production coordinator Karen Knapp established schedules and communicated production details to the printer, ensuring a timely product. And Dianne Woo brought her proofreading skills to a late version of the text. Kudos to each and all.

We thank the artists for their participation in this presentation, as we do all of the lenders. We especially thank lenders Anne Cohen, president of the Glass Alliance of Los Angeles, for introductions and referrals to numerous other lenders; Saul E. Levi and Marsha N. Levine for underwriting the exhibition's opening reception; and Dale and Doug Anderson for their additional support of this project.

Our deepest thanks and gratitude go to Dan Greenberg and Susan Steinhauser, principal sponsors of the exhibition and its catalogue, and long-time patrons of LACMA, who have been the most ardent and loyal—and patient—supporters. Their good cheer and enlightened patronage have inspired every phase of this project. And their generous gifts of objects and funds over nearly a decade and a half have provided the foundation for LACMA's strong and still-growing collection of contemporary glass art. We are grateful for their support as both sponsors and lenders.

As co-curators, we would be remiss and falsely modest if we did not thank each other. Our two years' worth of numberless cross-country e-mails and telephone conversations were punctuated with occasional weeks of visits to private collections, intense periods of organization and decision making, and more than a few excellent meals and bottles of wine. In short, we had a great time together. We trust that our enthusiasm for the art in this show and the efforts of all connected with it carries through to its audience.

Howard N. Fox
Curator of Contemporary Art
Los Angeles County Museum of Art

Sarah Nichols
Chief Curator and Curator of Decorative Arts
Carnegie Museum of Art, Pittsburgh

CHECKLIST

Page numbers of illustrations are given in brackets. Object information is as supplied by the lenders. Dimensions are height x width x depth.

HANK MURTA ADAMS

(United States, b. 1956)

Fernando, c. 2001 [60]

Cast glass, copper

29 x 17 x 18 in. (73.7 x 43.2 x 45.7 cm)

Collection of Ellis and Lillian Berkowitz, Beverly Hills

MICHAEL ASCHENBRENNER

(United States, b. 1949)

Graduation Gowns Lay in Rags at Their Feet, from the Damaged Bone series, 1980–86 [114]

Glass, twigs, cloth, wire

Overall dimensions (approx.):

93 x 123 in. (236.2 x 312.4 cm)

Los Angeles County Museum of Art

Gift of the artist, courtesy of Cuttress Gallery, Pomona, California

M.2003.140a-y

LARRY BELL

(United States, b. 1939)

Cube, 1966 [23]

Vacuum-coated glass

12 3/16 x 12 3/16 x 12 3/16 in.

(30.8 x 30.8 x 30.8 cm)

Los Angeles County Museum of Art

Gift of Frederick R. Weisman Company

M.82.112.2

HOWARD BEN TRÉ

(United States, b. 1949)

Eleventh Figure, 1988 [64]

Sandcast glass

54 1/2 x 15 x 13 in. (138.4 x 38.1 x 33 cm)

Collection of Daniel Greenberg and Susan Steinhauser, Los Angeles

HOWARD BEN TRÉ

(United States, b. 1949)

Urn 4, 1990 [63]

Sandcast glass, lead, steel, aluminum

23 x 13 x 15 in. (58.4 x 33 x 38.1 cm)

Los Angeles County Museum of Art

Gift of Daniel Greenberg and Susan Steinhauser

AC1997.249.9

LYNDA BENGLIS

(United States, b. 1941)

MI, 1984 [80]

Glass, sandcast, powdered; ceramic oxides, metal inclusions

13 1/2 x 17 x 16 in.

(34.3 x 43.2 x 40.6 cm)

Los Angeles County Museum of Art

Gift of Daniel Greenberg and Susan Steinhauser

M.86.273.1

LYNDA BENGLIS

(United States, b. 1941)

Emmett, 1993 [81]

Cast glass

20 x 17 x 16 in.

(50.8 x 43.2 x 40.6 cm)

Collection of Marvin H. and Anne B. Cohen, Los Angeles

STANISLAW BOROWSKI

(France, b. 1944, active Poland)

Ship of Fools: Sail Away, 2001 [94]

Glass

27 x 24 1/2 x 7 in.

(68.6 x 62.2 x 17.8 cm)

Collection of Ellie and Mark Lainer, Encino, California

ROBERT CARLSON

(United States, b. 1952)

Quan-Yin, 1993 [92]

Blown glass, enamel, gilding

39 x 10 x 10 in.

(99.1 x 25.4 x 25.4 cm)

Los Angeles County Museum of Art

Gift of Daniel Greenberg and Susan

Steinhauser

AC1994.162.1

DALE CHIHULY

(United States, b. 1941)

Basket Cylinder, c. 1976 [32]

Glass

Height: 11¾ in (29.9 cm);

diameter: 5¼ in. (13.3 cm)

Los Angeles County Museum of Art

Gift of Daniel Greenberg and Susan

Steinhauser

AC1997.249.1

DANIEL CLAYMAN

(United States, b. 1957)

Untitled, 2001 [65]

Cast glass, bronze

14 x 30 x 20 in. (35.6 x 76.2 x 50.8 cm)

Collection of Marvin H. and Anne B.

Cohen, Los Angeles

TONY CRAGG

(England, b. 1949)

Eye Bath, 1986 [112]

Glass

9 ³/₈ x 9 ⁷/₈ x 9 ⁷/₈ in.

(23.8 x 25.1 x 25.1 cm)

Los Angeles County Museum of Art

Gift of Ann and Aaron Nisenson in

memory of Michael Nisenson

AC1995.183.14

TONY CRAGG

(England, b. 1949)

Mortar and Pestle, 1986 [113]

Glass

Mortar height: 6 in. (15.2 cm);

diameter: 8 in. (20.3 cm);

pestle length: 16¼ in. (41.3 cm)

Los Angeles County Museum of Art

Gift of Ann and Aaron Nisenson in

memory of Michael Nisenson

AC1995.183.13.1-.2

DAN DAILEY

(United States, b. 1947)

Woman Offering Water to a

Porcupine, 1981 [57]

Glass

9 ¹³/₁₆ x 7 ¹³/₁₆ in. (24.8 x 19.7 cm)

Los Angeles County Museum of Art

Gift of Daniel Greenberg and Susan

Steinhauser

M.86.273.2

DAN DAILEY

(United States, b. 1947)

Pompadour, 2004 [59]

Blown glass, sandblasted and acid-

polished

24 ½ x 16 x 8 ½ in.

(62.2 x 40.6 x 21.6 cm)

Collection of Sam and Nancy Kunin,

Tarzana, California

EINAR DE LA TORRE

(Mexico, b. 1963, active United States)

JAMEX DE LA TORRE

(Mexico, b. 1960, active United States)

Alchemy, 1996 [105]

Blown glass, mixed mediums

40 x 26 x 9 in. (101.6 x 66 x 22.9 cm)

Courtesy of Daniel Saxon Gallery,

West Hollywood, California

EINAR DE LA TORRE

(Mexico, b. 1963, active United States)

JAMEX DE LA TORRE

(Mexico, b. 1960, active United States)

Narcochic (celebrating the nouveau-

rich aesthetic of the narco-drug

traffickers in Mexico and Miami),

2003 [104]

Blown glass and mixed mediums on

aluminum panel

48 x 48 x 7 in. (121.9 x 121.9 x 17.8 cm)

Fisher Gallery, University of Southern

California, Purchase Fund

LAURA DE SANTILLANA

(Italy, b. 1955)

Mud, 2001 [35]

Handblown glass

14 ¼ x 15 ¼ x 2 ¼ in.

(36.2 x 38.7 x 5.7 cm)

Private collection, New York

LAURA DE SANTILLANA

(Italy, b. 1955)

Dawn III, 2002 [34]

Handblown and shaped glass

15 ¾ x 18 ⅛ x 2 ¼ in.

(40 x 46 x 5.7 cm)

Barry Friedman Ltd., New York

WIM DELVOYE

(Belgium, b. 1965)

Erato, from The 9 Muses series, 2001–2

[not depicted]

Glass, x-ray images, lead, steel

78 ¾ x 31 ½ in. (200 x 80 cm)

Courtesy of Olga Korper Gallery, Toronto

MICHAEL GLANCY

(United States, b. 1950)

Molecular TGE, 1984 [135]

Blown glass, industrial plate glass, copper, silver

7 ½ x 12 x 12 in. (19.1 x 30.5 x 30.5 cm)

Los Angeles County Museum of Art

Gift of Daniel Greenberg and Susan Steinhauser

M.86.273.3a-e

MICHAEL GLANCY

(United States, b. 1950)

Incognito Ruby Guardian, 1988 [136]

Engraved blown glass, engraved blue industrial plate glass, copper, gold

10 x 10 x 10 in. (25.4 x 25.4 x 25.4 cm)

Collection of Daniel Greenberg and Susan Steinhauser, Los Angeles

MICHAEL GLANCY

(United States, b. 1950)

UV Expansion, 1994 [137]

Engraved blown glass, industrial plate glass, copper

10 x 21 x 21 in. (25.4 x 53.3 x 53.3 cm)

Collection of Daniel Greenberg and Susan Steinhauser, Los Angeles

MICHAEL GLANCY

(United States, b. 1950)

Infinite Obsessions, 1999 [138]

Engraved blown glass, industrial plate glass, copper

13 x 18 x 18 in. (33 x 45.7 x 45.7 cm)

Collection of Daniel Greenberg and Susan Steinhauser, Los Angeles

MICHAEL GLANCY

(United States, b. 1950)

Biomorphic Ganglia, 2003 [139]

Engraved blown glass, industrial plate glass, copper

12 x 24 x 10 in. (30.5 x 61 x 25.4 cm)

Collection of Daniel Greenberg and Susan Steinhauser, Los Angeles

DIANE HOBSON

(England, b. 1943)

Vessel, 1988 [74]

Pâte de verre

5 x 3 x 2 ½ in. (12.7 x 7.6 x 6.4 cm)

Los Angeles County Museum of Art

Gift of Daniel Greenberg and Susan Steinhauser in honor of the museum's twenty-fifth anniversary

M.90.93.3

DIANE HOBSON

(England, b. 1943)

Vessel, c. 1987 [75]

Pâte de verre

5 ¾ x 5 ⅜ x 4 ¾ in.

(14.6 x 13.7 x 12.1 cm)

Collection of Daniel Greenberg and Susan Steinhauser, Los Angeles

TOSHIO IEZUMI

(Japan, b. 1954)

Ring of Water, 1995 [29]

Glass, laminated and polished

Height: 3 ¾ in. (9.5 cm);

diameter: 25 ¾ in. (65.4 cm)

Los Angeles County Museum of Art

Gift of Daniel Greenberg and Susan Steinhauser

M.2001.79

SILVIA LEVENSON

(Argentina, b. 1957, active Italy)

Pink Cinderella, 2000 [107]

Glass, metal tacks

Each: 3 ¾ x 2 ¾ x 8 ¾ in.

(9.5 x 7 x 22.2 cm)

Collection of Daniel Greenberg and Susan Steinhauser, Los Angeles

SILVIA LEVENSON

(Argentina, b. 1957, active Italy)

Sogni Sospesi (Suspended Dreams), from the Trans-Ferirsi series, 1995 [108]

Kiln-cast glass, cord

11 7/8 x 9 7/16 x 1 9/16 in. (30 x 24 x 4 cm)

Collection of Ellie and Mark Lainer, Encino, California

SHERRIE LEVINE

(United States, b. 1947)

Crystal Newborn, 1993 [128]

Cast glass, sandblasted

5 x 8 x 8 1/2 in. (12.7 x 20.3 x 21.6 cm)

Los Angeles County Museum of Art

Gift of Daniel Greenberg and Susan Steinhauser

AC1997.249.31

SHERRIE LEVINE

(United States, b. 1947)

Black Newborn, 1994 [129]

Cast glass, sandblasted

5 x 8 x 8 1/2 in. (12.7 x 20.3 x 21.6 cm)

Los Angeles County Museum of Art

Purchased with funds provided by Daniel Greenberg and Susan Steinhauser

AC1995.87.1

STANISLAV LIBENSKÝ

(Czechoslovakia, b. 1921)

JAROSLAVA BRYCHTOVÁ

(Czechoslovakia, b. 1924)

Arcus I, 1990 [69]

Cast glass, sandblasted and hand-polished

33 1/16 x 37 1/16 x 6 1/2 in. (83.9 x 94.1 x 16.5 cm)

Collection of Daniel Greenberg and Susan Steinhauser, Los Angeles

STANISLAV LIBENSKÝ

(Czechoslovakia, b. 1921)

JAROSLAVA BRYCHTOVÁ

(Czechoslovakia, b. 1924)

Green Eye of the Pyramid, 1993 [68]

Glass

33 1/8 x 38 5/8 x 6 3/4 in. (84.1 x 98.1 x 17.2 cm)

Los Angeles County Museum of Art

Gift of Daniel Greenberg and Susan Steinhauser

AC1997.249.27

VĔRA LIŠKOVÁ

(Czechoslovakia, 1924–1985)

Music, 1980 [16]

Glass, blown and lampworked

24 x 24 x 20 in. (61 x 61 x 50.8 cm)

Los Angeles County Museum of Art

Gift of Werner Boeninger

M.87.197

HARVEY LITTLETON

(United States, b. 1922)

Red/Blue Combination Arc, 1984 [31]

Glass

14 x 15 x 2 in. (35.6 x 38.1 x 5.1 cm)

Los Angeles County Museum of Art

Gift of Daniel Greenberg and Susan Steinhauser

AC1997.249.12.1-.2

JESSICA LOUGHLIN

(Australia, b. 1975)

Vertical Views 12, 2001 [28]

Glass

47 x 8 x 1 in. (119.4 x 20.3 x 2.5 cm)

Collection of Dr. Arthur Liu, Tarzana, California

FLORA MACE

(United States, b. 1949)

JOEY KIRKPATRICK

(United States, b. 1952)

Zanfirico Still Life, 1995 [56]

Blown glass

Dimensions of bowl: 2 x 15 x 15 in. (5.1 x 38.1 x 38.1 cm)

Collection of Dale and Doug Anderson, Palm Beach, Florida

IVAN MAREŠ

(Czechoslovakia, b. 1956)

Haystack, 1996 [77]

Kiln-cast glass

21 x 45 x 8 in. (53.3 x 114.3 x 20.3 cm)

Collection of Daniel Greenberg and Susan Steinhauser, Los Angeles

IVAN MAREŠ

(Czechoslovakia, b. 1956)

Nautilus, 1999 [76]

Cast glass

29 7/8 x 36 1/2 x 10 3/4 in. (75.9 x 92.7 x 27.3 cm)

Los Angeles County Museum of Art

Gift of Daniel Greenberg and Susan Steinhauser

M.2003.202

RICHARD MARQUIS

(United States, b. 1945)

American Acid Capsule with Cloth Container, 1969–70 [53]

Solid worked glass, murrine, a canno, and incalmo techniques

Glass capsule: 4 ¼ x 1 ¾ x 1 ¾ in. (10.8 x 4.5 x 4.5 cm); cloth bag: 7 x 3 ½ in. (17.8 x 8.9 cm)

Collection of Dale and Doug Anderson, Palm Beach, Florida; promised gift to Metropolitan Museum of Art, New York

RICHARD MARQUIS

(United States, b. 1945)

Teapot, #21 from the Fabricated Weird series, 1979 [54]

Blown, cut, polished, and reassembled glass

5 x 4 x 6 in. (12.7 x 10.2 x 15.2 cm)

Los Angeles County Museum of Art

Gift of Anita and Julius L. Zelman through the 1987 Collectors Committee

M.87.154

RICHARD MARQUIS

(United States, b. 1945)

D'Marquis Teapot Trophy, 1987–88 [51]

Blown glass, murrine technique, zanfirico handles

34 ½ x 11 x 7 ¼ in. (87.6 x 27.9 x 18.4 cm)

Collection of Dr. Arthur Liu, Tarzana, California

RICHARD MARQUIS

(United States, b. 1945)

Goblet Teapot, 1988 [52]

Blown glass

9 ½ x 4 x 3 ½ in. (24.1 x 10.2 x 8.9 cm)

Collection of Gloria and Sonny Kamm, Encino, California

RICHARD MARQUIS

(United States, b. 1945)

Marquiscarpa #38, 1992 [50]

Glass

8 x 12 ½ x 3 ⅛ in. (20.3 x 31.8 x 7.9 cm)

Los Angeles County Museum of Art

Gift of Daniel Greenberg and Susan Steinhauser

AC1997.249.4

RITA MCBRIDE

(United States, b. 1960)

Chair, 1997 (edition 1/3) [122]

Murano glass, plastic wrap

35 ½ x 16 ¼ x 21 in. (90.2 x 41.3 x 53.3 cm)

Collection of Brenda Potter and Michael Sandler, Beverly Hills

JOSIAH MCELHENY

(United States, b. 1966)

Ornament and Crime, 2001–2 [130]

Blown glass, electric lights, oil on wood

Overall dimensions: 51 x 84 x 12 in. (129.5 x 213.4 x 30.5 cm)

Los Angeles County Museum of Art

Purchased with funds provided by Daniel Greenberg and Susan Steinhauser

RICHARD MEITNER

(United States, b. 1949, active Netherlands)

Progress IV, 1998 [100]

Blown and enameled glass

17 ¾ x 23 ½ x 8 in. (45.1 x 59.7 x 20.3 cm)

Barry Friedman Ltd., New York

RICHARD MEITNER

(United States, b. 1949, active Netherlands)

Branch, 2001 [101]

Blown and enameled glass, oxidized iron, lampworked glass

Height: 31 ¾ in. (80.7 cm)

Barry Friedman Ltd., New York

KLAUS MOJE

(Germany, b. 1936, active Australia)

11-1983 #18, 1986 [39]

Glass

20 x 21 x 3 in. (50.8 x 53.3 x 7.6 cm)

Los Angeles County Museum of Art

Gift of Daniel Greenberg and Susan Steinhauser

AC1997.249.20

KLAUS MOJE

(Germany, b. 1936, active Australia)

2-1990 #9, 1990 [41]

Mosaic glass, fused and slumped, wheel-ground

13 x 13 x 2 in. (33 x 33 x 5.1 cm)

Collection of Daniel Greenberg and Susan Steinhauser, Los Angeles

KLAUS MOJE

(Germany, b. 1936, active Australia)

7-1990 #31, 1990 [43]

Mosaic glass

17 x 18 x 2 ½ in. (43.2 x 45.7 x 6.4 cm)

Collection of Daniel Greenberg and

Susan Steinhauser, Los Angeles

KLAUS MOJE

(Germany, b. 1936, active Australia)

4-1994 #34, 1994 [42]

Mosaic glass

17 ¼ x 17 ¼ x 2 ½ in.

(43.8 x 43.8 x 6.4 cm)

Collection of Daniel Greenberg and

Susan Steinhauser, Los Angeles

KLAUS MOJE

(Germany, b. 1936, active Australia)

Untitled #48, 1995 [40]

Glass

2 ¾ x 12 ¾ x 8 ½ in.

(7 x 32.2 x 21.6 cm)

Los Angeles County Museum of Art

Gift of Daniel Greenberg and Susan

Steinhauser

AC1997.249.21

WILLIAM MORRIS

(United States, b. 1957)

Burial Raft, 1991 [84–5]

Glass

8 x 21 x 8 in. (20.3 x 53.3 x 20.3 cm)

Collection of Saul E. Levi and Marsha

N. Levine, Los Angeles

WILLIAM MORRIS

(United States, b. 1957)

Dahl Sheep, 2001–2 [83]

Glass

36 x 20 x 15 in. (91.4 x 50.8 x 38.1 cm)

Richard and Diane Fisher, Malibu,

California

JAY MUSLER

(United States, b. 1949)

Cityscape, 1982 [92]

Glass

Height: 7 ½ in. (19.1 cm);

diameter: 18 in. (45.7 cm)

Los Angeles County Museum of Art

Gift of Daniel Greenberg and Susan

Steinhauser

M.86.273.8

JAY MUSLER

(United States, b. 1949)

Karma Coma, 1999 [91]

Glass, oil paint

48 x 29 x 12 in. (121.9 x 73.7 x 30.5 cm)

Collection of Marilyn and Sam

Benton, Los Angeles

JOEL PHILIP MYERS

(United States, b. 1934)

Cfbyekkksg, 1984 [37]

Glass

7 ¼ x 15 x 3 ¼ in. (18.4 x 38.1 x 8.3 cm)

Los Angeles County Museum of Art

Gift of Daniel Greenberg and Susan

Steinhauser

AC1997.249.5

JOEL PHILIP MYERS

(United States, b. 1934)

Cforangeredksg, 1988 [36]

Glass

27 ¾ x 26 x 4 ½ in. (70.5 x 66 x 11.4

cm)

Los Angeles County Museum of Art

Gift of John and Maxine Gano Mayo

AC1994.84.1

BRUCE NAUMAN

(United States, b. 1941)

Human Nature / Life Death / Knows

Doesn't Know, 1983 [141]

Neon, glass

107 ½ x 107 x 5 ¹³⁄₁₆ in.

(273.1 x 271.8 x 14.6 cm)

Los Angeles County Museum of Art

Modern and Contemporary Art

Council Fund

M.84.36

JORGE PARDO

(Cuba, b. 1963, active United States)

Untitled, 2001 [47]

Handblown glass, lighting fixtures,

electrical wiring

Three lamps, each height: 14 ½ in.

(36.8 cm); diameter: 7 ½ in. (19.1 cm)

Los Angeles County Museum of Art

Purchased with funds provided by

Daniel Greenberg and Susan

Steinhauser

M2002.226a-c

THOMAS PATTI

(United States, b. 1943)

Starfire Four-Ringed Echo with Azurlite, Red, and Green, 1994 [24]

Glass

4 5/16 x 5 31/32 x 4 1/2 in.

(11 x 15.2 x 11.4 cm)

Collection of the artist

THOMAS PATTI

(United States, b. 1943)

Modulated Gray with Orange, Blue, Green, 2002 [25]

Glass, metal

13 3/8 x 10 1/4 x 2 1/2 in.

(34 x 26 x 6.4 cm)

Collection of Jeffrey and Cynthia Manocherian, New York

FLO PERKINS

(United States, b. 1951)

My Third Arid Dream, 1981–82 [61]

Blown glass, silicone

Height: 8–21 in. (20.3–53.3 cm)

Los Angeles County Museum of Art Gift of Daniel Greenberg and Susan Steinhauser

AC1997.249.15.1-.12

CLIFFORD RAINEY

(Northern Ireland, b. 1948, active United States)

Hollow Torso, No Step Is Final, 2000–1 [116]

Glass, Napa River stone, maple, iron, chain, C-clamps, gold leaf, pigment

34 1/2 x 12 in. (87.6 x 30.5 cm)

Los Angeles County Museum of Art Purchased with funds provided by the Glass Alliance of Los Angeles and the Decorative Arts Council

M.2001.152.1-.3

CLIFFORD RAINEY

(Northern Ireland, b. 1948, active United States)

Caryatid, 2003 [117]

Lead crystal, steel

Two units: 43 x 12 x 12 in.

(109.2 x 30.5 x 30.5 cm);

28 x 12 x 12 in. (71.1 x 30.5 x 30.5 cm)

Collection of Richard Sloan, Tarzana, California

SETH RANDAL

(United States, b. 1957)

Fit for a Queen, 1998 [86]

Cast crystal, copper, gold, enclosed lighting fixtures

Two units: 38 x 8 x 10 in.

(96.5 x 20.3 x 25.4 cm);

28 x 8 x 9 in. (71.1 x 20.3 x 22.9 cm)

Collection of Marvin H. and Anne B. Cohen, Los Angeles

JILL REYNOLDS

(United States, b. 1956)

Replicate, 2003 [132–3]

Glass, rubber tubing

13 x 15 1/2 x 8 in. (33 x 39.4 x 20.3 cm)

Carnegie Museum of Art, Pittsburgh; Second Century Acquisition Fund, 2004

GINNY RUFFNER

(United States, b. 1952)

Beauty as Medusa, 1990 [96]

Lampworked glass, sandblasted and painted

18 3/8 in. (46.7 cm)

Collection of Marvin H. and Anne B. Cohen, Los Angeles

GINNY RUFFNER

(United States, b. 1952)

Beauty's Alter Ego as a Tornado, 1990 [97]

Glass, paint

18 x 11 x 11 in. (45.7 x 28 x 28 cm)

Los Angeles County Museum of Art Gift of Brendan Walter and Ginny Ruffner

M.91.18

GINNY RUFFNER

(United States, b. 1952)

Conceptual Narrative Morphing up the Evolutionary Ladder, 1998 [98]

Lampworked glass, mixed mediums

23 x 27 x 9 in. (58.4 x 68.6 x 22.9 cm)

Collection of Saul E. Levi and Marsha N. Levine, Los Angeles

JUDITH SCHAECHTER

(United States, b. 1961)

Dreams of the Fisherman's Wife, 2004 [109]

Stained glass in light-box

33 1/2 x 52 in. (85.1 x 132.1 cm)

Carnegie Museum of Art, Pittsburgh; Ailsa Mellon Bruce Fund, 2005

KIKI SMITH

(Germany, b. 1954, active United States)

Tombs, 1989 [120]

Fired and mirrored glass, wood shelf

Overall dimensions: 48 x 96 in.

(121.9 x 243.8 cm)

Los Angeles County Museum of Art

Purchased with funds provided by Daniel Greenberg and Susan Steinhauser

AC1997.163.1.1-.22

THERMAN STATOM

(United States, b. 1953)

Rey de Sol Mexico, 1988 [124]

Glass, paint

21 x 13 x 11½ in. (53.3 x 33 x 29.2 cm)

Los Angeles County Museum of Art

Gift of Daniel Greenberg and Susan Steinhauser

AC1997.249.16

THERMAN STATOM

(United States, b. 1953)

Ladder, c. 1988 [125]

Glass

Ladder: 77 x 14 x 3¼ in.

(195.6 x 35.6 x 8.3 cm);

base: 1½ x 24 x 12 in.

(3.8 x 61 x 30.5 cm)

Collection of Gloria and Sonny Kamm, Encino, California

LINO TAGLIAPIETRA

(Italy, b. 1934)

Boat, 1998 [27]

Blown glass with hammered finish

7 x 72 x 7 in. (17.8 x 182.9 x 17.8 cm)

Collection of Saul E. Levi and Marsha N. Levine, Los Angeles

KARLA TRINKLEY

(United States, b. 1956)

Tut, 1984 [72]

Glass

9½ x 9¾ 10 in.

(24.1 x 24.8 x 25.4 cm)

Los Angeles County Museum of Art

Gift of Daniel Greenberg and Susan Steinhauser

AC1997.249.8

KARLA TRINKLEY

(United States, b. 1956)

El Tajin, 1985 [71]

Glass

Height: 8 in. (20.3 cm);

diameter: 9 in. (22.9 cm)

Los Angeles County Museum of Art

Gift of Daniel Greenberg and Susan Steinhauser

M.86.273.12

KARLA TRINKLEY

(United States, b. 1956)

Peela Peela Birdboat, 1994 [73]

Glass, poplar, cedar, graphite, metal

36 x 25 x 12 in.

(91.4 x 63.5 x 30.5)

Los Angeles County Museum of Art

Gift of Daniel Greenberg and Susan Steinhauser

AC1997.249.18

BERTIL VALLIEN

(Sweden, b. 1938)

P1-84 Boat, 1984 [90]

Glass

19½ x 5 x 3 in.

(49.5 x 12.7 x 7.6 cm)

Los Angeles County Museum of Art

Gift of Daniel Greenberg and Susan Steinhauser

AC1997.249.29

BERTIL VALLIEN

(Sweden, b. 1938)

Watcher V-03, 2003 [90]

Glass

76 x 12 x 5½ in.

(193 x 30.5 x 14 cm)

Collection of Richard and Diane Fisher, Malibu, California

BERTIL VALLIEN

(Sweden, b. 1938)

Head, 1997 [89]

Glass with metal inclusions
mounted on wood post mounted
on metal base

Head: 9 x 8 x 10 in.
(22.9 x 20.3 x 25.4 cm);

overall dimensions: 72½ x 14 x 14 in.
(184.2 x 35.6 x 35.6 cm)

Collection of Dale and Doug
Anderson, Palm Beach, Florida

FRANTIŠEK VÍZNER

(Czechoslovakia, b. 1936)

Object III, 1989 [66]

Glass

Diameter: 11½ in. (29.2 cm)

Los Angeles County Museum of Art
Gift of Daniel Greenberg and Susan
Steinhauser

AC1997.249.30

FRANTIŠEK VÍZNER

(Czechoslovakia, b. 1936)

Bowl, 1994 [67]

Cast glass

Height: 3¼ in. (8.3 cm);
diameter: 11½ in. (29.2 cm)

Collection of Jeffrey and Cynthia
Manocherian, New York

JACK WAX

(United States, b. 1954)

Issue, 1998 [78]

Glass, pigment, adhesive

7 x 15 x 9 in. (17.8 x 38.1 x 22.9 cm)

Los Angeles County Museum of Art
Purchased with funds provided by
the Glass Alliance of Los Angeles
and the Decorative Arts Council

AC1999.169.1.1-.2

PAE WHITE

(United States, b. 1963)

Untitled site-specific installation,
2006 [not depicted]

Blown mirrored glass

Dimensions to be determined

Lent by the artist and 1301 PE, Los
Angeles

ROBERT WILLSON

(United States, 1912–2000)

Ranch Totem, 1983 [88]

Glass

16 3/8 x 6 3/4 x 5 in.
(41.6 x 17.1 x 12.7 cm)

Los Angeles County Museum of Art
Gift of Margaret Pace Willson

M.2001.166

CHRISTOPHER WILMARTH

(United States, 1943–1987)

Gnomon's Parade (Place), 1980 [28]

Glass, steel

96 x 40 x 35 ½ in.
(243.8 x 101.6 x 90.2 cm)

Carnegie Museum of Art,
Pittsburgh; The Henry L. Hillman
Fund and Carnegie International
Fund, 1982

ANN WOLFF

(Sweden, b. 1937)

Outside the Kitchen, c. 1982 [102]

Sheet glass

28 1/8 x 23 1/4 in. (71.3 x 59 cm)

Los Angeles County Museum of Art
Gift of Daniel Greenberg and Susan
Steinhauser

M. 84.201.2

TOOTS ZYNSKY

(United States, b. 1951)

Chaos in Paradise, 1995 [45]

Glass threads, fused

8 x 16 x 8 in. (20.3 x 40.6 x 20.3 cm)

Collection of Dale and Doug
Anderson, Palm Beach, Florida

TOOTS ZYNSKY

(United States, b. 1951)

Scalmana, 2003 [44]

Glass threads, fused

11 x 24 x 12 ½ in. (27.9 x 61 x 31.8 cm)

Collection of Dale and Doug
Anderson, Palm Beach, Florida

ARCHITECTURE

(These works were represented photographically in the exhibition.)

JAMES CARPENTER
(United States, b. 1949)
JAMES CARPENTER DESIGN ASSOCIATES
Lens Ceiling, 2000 [148]
Phoenix Federal Building, Phoenix, Arizona

DALE CHIHULY
(United States, b. 1941)
Fiori di Como, 1998 [144–5]
Bellagio Hotel, Las Vegas, Nevada

SIR NORMAN FOSTER
(England, b. 1935)
FOSTER AND PARTNERS
30 St. Mary Axe, 2004 [153]
London, England

ZAHA HADID
(Iraq, b. 1950)
ZAHA HADID ARCHITECTS
Proposal for 2012 New York City Olympic Village, 2004 [158]

REM KOOLHAAS
(Netherlands, b. 1944)
OFFICE FOR METROPOLITAN ARCHITECTURE
Seattle Public Library, 2004 [156–7]
Seattle, Washington

ERIC OWEN MOSS
(United States, b. 1943)
ERIC OWEN MOSS ARCHITECTS
The Umbrella, 1999 [152]
Culver City, California

RENZO PIANO
(Italy, b. 1937)
RENZO PIANO & BUILDING WORKSHOP
London Bridge Tower,
work in progress [154]
London, England

INGALILL WAHLROOS-RITTER
(United States, b. 1965)
SMITH-MILLER + HAWKINSON
Corning Museum of Glass renovation, 2001 [149]
Corning, New York

LENDERS TO THE EXHIBITION

Dale and Doug Anderson

Marilyn and Sam Benton

Ellis and Lillian Berkowitz

Marvin H. and Anne B. Cohen

Richard and Diane Fisher

Daniel Greenberg and Susan Steinhauser

Gloria and Sonny Kamm

Sam and Nancy Kunin

Ellie and Mark Lainer

Saul E. Levi and Marsha N. Levine

Dr. Arthur Liu

Jeffrey and Cynthia Manocherian

Thomas Patti

Brenda Potter and Michael Sandler

Private collection

Richard Sloan

Pae White

Carnegie Museum of Art, Pittsburgh

Fisher Gallery, University of Southern California

Barry Friedman Ltd., New York

Olga Korper Gallery, Toronto

Los Angeles County Museum of Art

Daniel Saxon Gallery, West Hollywood, California

1301PE, Los Angeles

LOS ANGELES COUNTY BOARD OF SUPERVISORS, 2006

Gloria Molina
Supervisor, First District

Yvonne Brathwaite Burke
Supervisor, Second District

Zev Yaroslavsky
Supervisor, Third District

Don Knabe
Supervisor, Fourth District

Michael D. Antonovich
Supervisor, Fifth District

David E. Janssen
Chief Administrative Officer

LOS ANGELES COUNTY MUSEUM OF ART BOARD OF TRUSTEES, FISCAL YEAR 2005–2006

Nancy Daly Riordan
Chairman of the Board

Frank E. Baxter
Vice Chairman

Mrs. Stewart Resnick
Vice Chairman

Christopher V. Walker
Vice Chairman

Michael G. Smooke
Secretary

William Hayden Ahmanson
William Howard Ahmanson
Wallis Annenberg
William J. Bell, Jr.
Suzanne Deal Booth
Donald L. Bren
Eli Broad
Iris Cantor
Mrs. Edward W. Carter
Robert A. Day
Janet Dreisen
Jeremy G. Fair
Andrew Gordon
Andrew Hauptman
Enrique Hernandez, Jr.
John F. Hotchkis
Judith G. Jones
Robert A. Kotick
Mrs. Harry Lenart
Abby J. Levy
Robert Looker
Ms. Monica C. Lozano
Robert F. Maguire III
William A. Mingst
Mrs. Wendy Stark Morrissey
Jane Nathanson
Peter Norton
John P. Puerner

Tony Ressler
Edward P. Roski, Jr.
Robert Simonds
Donald Tang
Sandra W. Terner
James A. Thomas
Casey Wasserman

Senior Trustees

Mrs. Lionel Bell
Dr. George N. Boone
Mrs. William M. Carpenter
Camilla Chandler Frost
Stanley Grinstein
Mrs. Dwight M. Kendall

Life Trustees

Mrs. Howard Ahmanson
Robert H. Ahmanson
Robert O. Anderson
Daniel N. Belin
Julian Ganz, Jr.
Eric Lidow
Mrs. Lillian Apodaca Weiner
Walter L. Weisman